more Lovely Knitted Lace

more Lovely Knitted Lace

Contemporary Patterns in Geometric Shapes

Brooke Nico

LARK

New York

New York

An Imprint of Sterling Publishing
1166 Avenue of the Americas
New York, NY 10036

Text © 2016 Brooke Nico
Photography and Illustrations © 2016 by Lark Crafts

ISBN 978-1-4547-0918-3

Distributed in Canada by Sterling Publishing
c/o Canadian Manda Group, 664 Annette Street
Toronto, Ontario, Canada M6S 2C8
Distributed in the United Kingdom by GMC Distribution Services
Castle Place, 166 High Street, Lewes, East Sussex, England BN7 1XU
Distributed in Australia by Capricorn Link (Australia) Pty. Ltd.
P.O. Box 704, Windsor, NSW 2756, Australia

For information about custom editions, special sales, and premium and corporate purchases,
please contact Sterling Special Sales at 800-805-5489 or specialsales@sterlingpublishing.com.

Email academic@larkbooks.com for information about desk and examination copies.
The complete policy can be found at larkcrafts.com.

Photography by Carrie Hoge
Illustrations by Alexis Seabrook

Manufactured in China

2 4 6 8 10 9 7 5 3 1

larkcrafts.com

contents

Introduction...6

Getting Started 8

circles 19

Mozzetta Capelet...21

DeBauliver Top 27

Whorl Shawl 34

Aria Gauntlets...39

triangles 45

Arbor Triangular Shawl 47

Amaryllis Entrelac Shawl 55

Montauk Sweater...62

Peony Tam 69

squares 73

Holly Shawl 75

Keira Wrap..84

Wanderlust Shawl..89

Lea Sleeveless Top 93

rectangles...101

Uno Cowl 103

Primrose Tunic 104

Troika Wrap 113

Duo Vest 119

Knitting Abbreviations 124

Yarn Weights 125

Knitting Needle Size Chart...............................125

Acknowledgments..126

Index...127

About the Author..128

introduction

Welcome to the world of lace knitting. One of the things I love most about lace knitting is the wealth of possibilities it contains. No matter what your taste in knitting is, there's a lace knitting project for you.

Although very traditional lace projects often are worked in cobweb weight yarn on teeny tiny needles, not *all* lace knitting is, and therefore not all the projects in this book are. Consider Wanderlust, a great shawl option for those who prefer to work at a larger gauge. Worked in bulky weight wool, Wanderlust is a shawl created for warmth and coziness, big enough to envelop yourself in but lacy enough to look fashionable. Whether you prefer projects worked in the finest cobweb lace or crave the immediate gratification of a bulkier yarn, you've got options—with several stops in between.

Shawls are lovely and fun to knit, but there does come a point (or so I'm told) where one has enough shawls. I have included several shawls and other smaller accessories, including gauntlets, scarves, and a hat. But for those of you ready for a bigger challenge, I've also included some larger-scale garments: sweaters, capes, and even a dress. One advantage of lace knitting is that the fabric does most of the work for the design, and so a simple silhouette is often best—coincidentally, that means less work

for you when it comes to shaping. Lea is an example of this kind of simple shape (a rectangle for the yoke and two squares for the body), but when it is combined with an easy-to-master lace motif, that simple shape creates a fabulous garment.

For knitters who prefer working in shorter bursts, I've played a bit with modular pieces in this book. Amaryllis is a triangle shawl that is worked entrelac-style. DeBauliver and Holly both are knit in strips. Modular knitting allows you to break the knitting up into small bits, making a larger project feel more manageable. (In Amaryllis, for example, each entrelac diamond takes only a couple of hours to knit.) The other advantage of modular knitting is that you bind off each section as you complete it. That means that every few hours you get to spread your work out, admire it, and give yourself a big pat on the back for having completed something! Try exploring your own lace motifs and inserting them in any of the modular pieces. DeBauliver is a great starting place because the final shape, a cone, leaves a little more wiggle room in the math.

I hope this book inspires you to explore all the available options in your lace knitting. Enjoy!

getting started

A Note on Yarn

Most of the yarns used in this book have at least some wool or other animal-derived (e.g., alpaca, mohair, bison) content. I prefer to use these yarns for lace knitting because of the body these protein-based fibers lend to the final fabric. A lace fabric inherently has less structure than a stockinette stitch fabric: All those holes want to stretch somehow. Wool's natural elasticity and the crimp of animal fibers help give lace fabric structure, keeping it from sagging and stretching out of shape. That structure is what keeps the shoulder seam sitting squarely on the shoulders (rather than drooping down to the elbows) and keeps the finished garment looking fresh as long as you wear it.

At times, I've deliberately sought to create more drape in a garment, as in the Mozzetta Capelet. In those cases, I looked for yarns that have some nonwool natural fiber content, such as silk or alpaca, fibers that tend to drape. For example, the wool/silk blend of Cascade's Venezia provides the best of both worlds, giving Mozzetta drape without droop. When I was designing DeBauliver, however, I fell in love with an all-silk yarn called Heaven's Hand Silke. Since there was no wool content to help stabilize the lace, I opted for modular construction as a way to add structure through the multiple seams.

In the end, however, my yarn recommendations are just that—only recommendations. Explore your own fiber options and knit with fibers you love. Hate wool? Try a cotton/wool blend or an alpaca/linen blend. My only recommendation is to make a large gauge swatch, block it well, and then hang it overnight to let it stretch, as it will when the garment is complete, to give you a sense of how the yarn will behave in the finished garment.

Gauge

As the owner of a knitting shop, I know all too well that no one likes to do a gauge swatch. Let's be honest: For a shawl, does it really matter if the finished piece is 62" wide rather than my 58"? Truth be told, quite often you can block a piece of lace knitting to almost any size you want it to be. One of the hardest things for me in writing lace patterns is deciding what gauge to give in the pattern. Do I stretch it a bit or a lot? What size holes will a typical knitter prefer? Can a knitter readily duplicate my gauge when using a different yarn?

For that reason, you will notice that many of the patterns in this book have a specified gauge that is more than the typical 4-inch gauge swatch. In lace knitting, the stitches expand and contract with every yarn over and decrease. In a larger motif, those changes take place over a bigger swath of knitting, and the gauge may not be consistent within the confines of 4 inches; this would result in an inaccurate measurement over a smaller swatch. I strongly encourage you to swatch diligently, with two or more repeats of a motif in your swatch, keeping an eye how the lace looks when it is blocked to the stated gauge. Is it too loose or open? Does it look sloppy or perhaps too rigid? If that is the case, adjust the needle size appropriately (go down a size or two if it's too loose, up a size or two if too rigid) and try again. (One added benefit of attentive swatching is that you'll become more familiar with the pattern stitches, helping you read your stitches more accurately and avoid mistakes when it comes time to knit the actual garment.)

That being said, for shawls and other unfitted accessories you are of course always free to adjust the finished size by adjusting the gauge to fit your needs.

Techniques

KNIT CAST ON

For most of my lace knitting, I like to use a knit cast-on technique. The first and most important reason is structural: Because you are knitting the stitches as you cast them on, the gauge of the cast-on row will match the gauge of the rest of the piece. Other cast-on methods often result in a cast-on row that is tighter than the rest of the knitting, and so it gathers in or is looser than the rest of the knitting and flares out. The second reason I prefer a knit cast on is practical. Often in lace knitting, you are casting on hundreds of stitches. If you are using a long-tail cast on, figuring out how long to leave the tail to accommodate all those stitches is a guessing game at best. With the knit cast on, however, a 4-inch tail is sufficient regardless of the length of the cast-on row. The third reason is appearance. A knit cast on leaves a sturdy chain underneath the cast-on row that isn't too bulky but looks attractive.

To do the knit cast on:

1. Make a slip knot and place it on the left needle. This is your first stitch.

2. *Knit the stitch but do not drop it off the left needle. (You will have the new stitch on the right needle and the original slip knot on the left needle.)

3. Hold the needles parallel.

4. Slip the new stitch knitwise onto the left needle.

5. Repeat from * until the required number of stitches is cast on.

In patterns for which I strongly believe that a particular cast-on method is best, I've specified that method in the instructions. If no cast-on method is specified, you can't go wrong by using the knit cast-on method.

YARN OVERS

Yarn overs are the go-to increase in lace knitting. To make a yarn over:

1. Bring the yarn to the front of the needles. If the last stitch was a knit stitch, the yarn needs to come to the front between the needles. If the last stitch was a purl stitch, the yarn is already at the front and doesn't need to move.

2. Pass the yarn over the top of the right needle, creating the yarn over.

3. Now get it into position to work the next stitch. If the next stitch is a knit stitch, the working yarn is already in back and you are good to go. If the next stitch is a purl stitch, the yarn needs to come to the front between the needles so that you are ready to purl.

The stitches immediately before and after the yarn over affect the kind of yarn over you'll make:

- To make a yarn over between two knit stitches, the yarn must travel around the right needle a full 360 degrees (from back, to front, and then to back again).

- For a yarn over between two purl stitches, the yarn also travels a full 360 degrees (from front to back and then to the front again).

- For a yarn over between a purl stitch and a knit stitch, the yarn travels less than 360 degrees (from front to back).

- For a yarn over between a knit stitch and a purl stitch, the yarn travels more than 360 degrees (from back to front, over the top to the back again, and then between the needles to the front).

You may notice the inevitable result of the different paths of yarn overs: In motifs that have yarn overs around reverse stockinette columns, as in Wanderlust, the holes on either side of the column will be different sizes. If this disparity bothers you, you can try to loosen the yarn over between the purl and the knit to make it larger, but that is difficult to do consistently.

The best solution is to make the yarn over between the knit and the purl smaller. Here's how to do it:

1. On right-side rows, when it comes time to make that yarn over, place a coilless safety pin on the working yarn at that spot. You are not making the yarn over at this point. The safety pin will sit at the spot where the yarn over should be. Continue on across the row. **(A)**

2. On the next row the safety pin is sitting on the strand of yarn that should create the yarn over. Pull on the safety pin slightly and place the yarn attached to the safety pin on the left needle to create the yarn over. Remove the safety pin and continue on. (**B**)

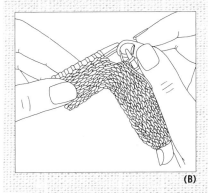

(B)

In DeBauliver, the edging is worked horizontal to the piece. In order To block the cape fully, every wrong-side row begins with "yo, p2tog" (this keeps that selvedge edge loose but tidy). Starting a row with a yarn over may seem a bit challenging at first, but it needn't be:

1. Hold the right needle behind the working yarn. (**C**)

2. Wrap the yarn 360 degrees counterclockwise around the right needle (**D**), creating one complete loop around the right needle. (**E**)

3. Now insert the right needle into the first two stitches purlwise and purl them together. (**F**)

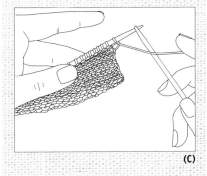

(C)

When you are working the right-side rows, remember that the last stitch you work should always be the first yarn over from the row before. That way you're more likely to notice it if you accidentally drop that yarn over (something that is easy to do).

CLUSTER STITCHES AND NUPPS

Cluster stitches are created when the knitter works into a group of stitches at the same time or works multiple times into the same stitch. Estonian stitch patterns in particular make use of many different types of cluster stitches. In my previous book, *Lovely Knitted Lace*, the Angel Shawl and Poinsettia Jacket feature a lovely water lily motif created with a cluster stitch. In this book, the Holly and Amaryllis shawls both feature a variation of a cluster stitch: the nupp.

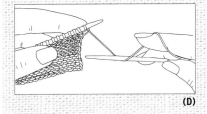

(D)

To make a nupp, you increase six times into a single stitch and work the original stitch, creating a cluster of seven stitches that arise out of that single original stitch. On the next row, the seven clustered stitches are knitted or purled together, taking you back to the single original stitch.

To work a nupp:

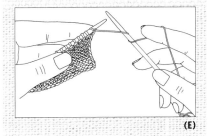

(E)

1. Into the next stitch work (k1, yo) three times and then knit into that stitch once more. Now drop the original stitch off the left needle and continue across the row.

2. Next row: Work across the row as indicated until you come to the nupp. Purl the next seven stitches together (or, if you are working in the round, knit those seven stitches together through the back loop).

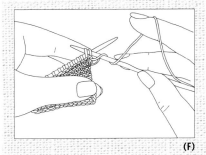

(F)

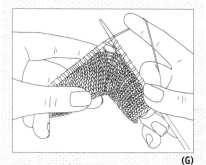

(G)

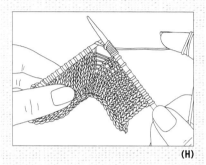

(H)

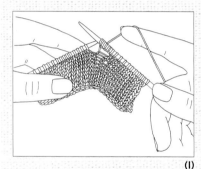

(I)

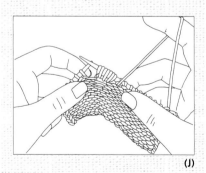

(J)

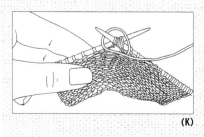

(K)

That p7tog (or k7tog tbl) can be really tight. To make my nupps easier to work, I like to loosen up that stitch by working double yarn overs, as follows:

1. *Insert the needle into the next stitch and knit it—*do not drop the stitch off the left needle*—and then make two yarn overs. (**G**)

2. Repeat from * twice more and then knit the stitch once more. (**H**)

3. Now you can drop the stitch off the left needle. You have ten new wraps around the right needle (four knit stitches and three double yarn overs). (**I**)

4. On the next row, when you come to the nupp, slip the stitches one at a time to the right needle, dropping the extra yarn overs (in other words, *slip one knit stitch, slip one yarn over, drop one yarn over * three times, slip last knit stitch), which puts you back to the seven required nupp stitches, each of which is a little elongated. (**J**)

5. Now you can easily p7tog (or k7tog tbl). (**K**)

The Mozzetta Capelet uses a simple cluster stitch called the Estonian star stitch. The star stitch used in Mozzetta requires you to work into a cluster of three original stitches rather than the one original stitch described above, performing each step by knitting the three original stitches together.

You will work (k3tog tbl, yo) twice and then another k3tog tbl, all in the same three original stitches, so that you create a cluster of five stitches out of the original three stitches. You can see that the stitch is called "5/3tbl" in the pattern, with the "5" indicating the cluster of stitches you created and the "3tbl" referring to the original stitches you worked the cluster into (3) by going into the back loop (tbl).

In charts, clusters usually are designated with a symbol like this:

The number on the bottom indicates the amount of stitches used to create the cluster, and the number on the top indicates the amount of stitches the cluster will create. This is the symbol used for Mozzetta's Estonian star stitch: (k3tog, yo) twice, then k3tog again, all into the same three original stitches, resulting in five stitches. On the next row, you'll decrease back to three stitches.

SHORT ROWS

In the Primrose Tunic, the asymmetric hem is created by working short rows. Short rows are just what they sound like: Instead of working across an entire row of stitches, you work only partway (the pattern gives you a specified number of stitches to work) and then turn your work, leaving the remaining stitches of the row unworked. Short rows create wedges in a piece of knitting, and in Primrose those wedges create the graceful lines of the hem.

You may have noticed when working short rows in the past that turning your knitting after working only a partial row can create a hole in the fabric. In a typical row of knitting, each stitch is connected to the stitches on either side of it. When you work short rows, if you do not somehow "connect" the last stitch worked before the turn to the stitch on its left, you'll see a hole. A wrap and turn (w&t) is used to connect the stitches and eliminate any hole. To wrap and turn:

1. On a knit row, work the required number of stitches. Slip the next stitch purlwise to the right needle. Bring the yarn to the front between the needles and then slip the stitch back to the left needle and bring the yarn to the back between the needles. You have "wrapped" the yarn around the stitch. Turn the work and begin the next row.

2. On a purl row, work the required number of stitches. Slip the next stitch purlwise to the right needle. Bring the yarn to the back between the needles and then slip the stitch back to the left needle, bringing the yarn to the front between the needles. Turn the work and begin the next row.

You will notice that the wraps leave a little purl bump underneath the wrapped stitch. This is fine in garter stitch or reverse stockinette stitch, where the bump blends in with the already nubbly fabric. But when you are working in regular stockinette stitch, such as Primrose, those purl bumps really stand out. Fortunately, there is an easy way to hide them. To hide wrapped stitches when you are working in stockinette stitch, do the following.

On a knit row:

1. Knit to the wrapped stitch. Slip the wrapped stitch to the right needle. (L)

2. Insert the left needle tip under the wrap and place it on the left needle. Slip the wrapped stitch back to the left needle and knit the wrap and stitch together with the working yarn. (M)

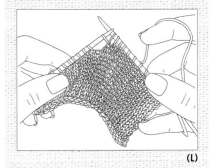

(L)

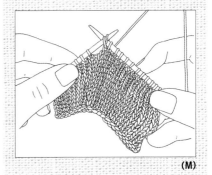

(M)

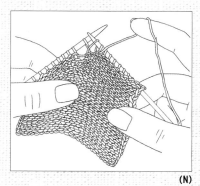

(N)

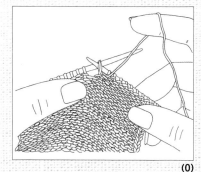

(O)

On a purl row:

1. To hide a wrap on a purl row, purl to the wrapped stitch. (**N**)

2. Insert the right needle tip into the wrap and place it on the left needle. Purl the wrap and stitch together with the working yarn. (**O**)

LACE BIND OFF

Lace knitting is extremely flexible and therefore sometimes requires a stretchier than normal bind off as is needed in Mozzetta Capelet. I like to use the lace bind off, otherwise known as a decrease bind off. This bind off essentially will add an extra little chain between the bind-off stitches. This chain can pop up if needed to stretch the fabric, but if it is not needed, it will hide just under the bind off.

To work the lace bind off:

1. Knit two stitches.

2. *Slip those two stitches back to the left-hand needle and knit them together through the back loop. You now have one stitch on the right-hand needle.

3. Knit one stitch, which puts you back to two stitches on the right needle.

4. Repeat from * across until you have worked all stitches off the left-hand needle. Fasten off the last stitch as usual.

circles

SOME WILL SAY THAT THE CIRCLE is the perfect shape, without beginning or end. One of the problems with circular shawls, however, is in the wearing of them. I have yet to find a great way to wear a circular shawl that really shows off all the lovely knitting. For that reason, in this chapter I chose to interpret the circle in other ways, as a cape, a top, a pair of gauntlets, and a fun swirl shawl. Each utilizes different methods for shaping the circle, so pick your favorite and have fun!

mozzetta capelet

THE TRADITIONAL "PI" SHAWL, as created by Elizabeth Zimmerman, is a center-out circular shawl that is shaped by doubling the stitches every time the rows are doubled. Mozzetta loosely interprets these instructions: Because we are creating a cape, a cone shape, rather than a shawl, which requires a nearly perfect circle to lie flat, we can play a little with the rate of increase. Knit from the top down, Mozzetta has 33 repeats of each lace motif. Each time you switch motifs, a few stitches are added to each repeat, and that creates the cape shape.

To block the hem out to a nice curve, I recommend using the lace bind off, which is explained in detail on page 16. Because of the nature of some of the lace motifs, particularly the cluster stitches, at times the stitches will need to cross over the marker lines. To do that, we employ a technique typically seen in doily construction and move the markers, starting the round on a new stitch.

SKILL LEVEL

INTERMEDIATE

FINISHED MEASUREMENTS

Circumference at lower hem 95"/241cm
Height 13"/33cm

MATERIALS AND TOOLS

Cascade Yarns Venezia Sport (70% merino, 30% silk; 3.5oz/100g = 307yd/281m): 2 skeins, color #159—approx 600yd/549m of worsted weight yarn (4)

Knitting needles: 4mm (size 6 U.S.) 24" circular needles or size to obtain gauge 3.5mm (size 4 U.S.) 16" circular needles or two sizes smaller than above

Stitch markers

Tapestry needle

GAUGE

Rows 39–60 of Chart 2 (8 sts/16 rows) = 2.25"/6cm wide by 3"/8cm tall, using larger needles after blocking
Always take time to check your gauge.

Special Abbreviations

4 into 1 decrease: Slip 2 sts together knitwise, k2tog, pass the 2 slipped stitches over this stitch. 4 stitches decreased into 1 stitch.

PATTERN STITCHES

chart 1: (see page 24)

RND 19: Move marker 1 st to left, *(K1, yo) twice, k2, rep from * to end of rnd—198 sts.

RND 20 & all even-numbered rnds: Knit.

RND 21, 23, & 25: *K2tog, yo, k1, yo, ssk, k1, rep from * to end of rnd.

RND 27: *5/3 tbl, yo, k1, yo, rep from * to end of rnd.

RND 29: Move marker 2 sts to left, then *k2tog, yo, k1, yo, ssk, k1, rep from * to end of rnd.

RND 31, 33, & 35: *K2tog, yo, k1, yo, ssk, k1, rep from * to end of rnd.

Rnd 37: *5/3 tbl, yo, k1, 1 yo, rep from * to end of rnd.

chart 2: (see page 24)

Row 39: Move marker 1 st to left, then *k1, yo, k5, yo, rep from * to end of rnd—264 sts.

Row 41: *K2, yo, ssk, k1, k2tog, yo, k1, rep from * to end of rnd.

Row 43: *K3, yo, sk2p, yo, k2, rep from * to end of rnd.

Row 45, 47, 49, 51, & 53: *K1, ssk, (k1, yo) twice, k1, k2tog, rep from * to end of rnd.

Row 55: *K1, yo, ssk, k3, k2tog, yo, rep from * to end of rnd.

Row 57: *K2, yo, ssk, k1, k2tog, yo, k1, rep from * to end of rnd.

Row 59: *K3, yo, sk2p, yo, k2, rep from * to end of rnd.

Row 61: *Yo, k1, yo, ssk, (k1, yo) twice, k1, k2tog, rep from * to end of rnd—330 sts.

Row 63: *K3, yo, ssk, (k1, yo) twice, k1, k2tog, yo, rep from * to end of rnd—396 sts.

Row 65: *Sk2p, yo, k1, k2tog, yo, k3, yo, ssk, k1, yo, rep from * to end of rnd.

chart 3: (see page 24)

Row 67 (RS): *K2, k2tog, yo, k5, yo, ssk, k1, rep from * to end of rnd—396 sts.

Row 69: *K1, k2tog, yo, k7, yo, ssk, rep from * to end of rnd.

Row 71: Move marker 1 st to right, then *sk2p, yo, k4, yo, ssk, k3, yo, rep from * to end of rnd.

Row 73: *Yo, ssk, k2, k2tog, yo, k1, yo, ssk, k3, rep from * to end of rnd.

Row 75: *Yo, ssk, k1, k2tog, yo, k3, yo, ssk, k2, rep from * to end of rnd.

Row 77: *Yo, ssk, k3, yo, sk2p, yo, k4, rep from * to end of rnd.

Row 79: *K1, yo, ssk, k3, yo, ssk, k2, k2tog, yo, rep from * to end of rnd.

Row 81: *(Yo, ssk) twice, k2, yo, ssk, k1, k2tog, yo, k1, rep from * to end of rnd.

Row 83: *K1, (yo, ssk) twice, k1, yo, ssk, (k2tog, yo) twice, rep from * to end of rnd.

Row 87: *(Yo, ssk) three times, yo, sk2p, yo, k2tog, yo, k1, rep from * to end of rnd.

Notes:
Capelet is knit in the round from the top down.

INSTRUCTIONS

neckband

Using smaller needles, CO 165 sts. Place marker and join to work in the round, being careful not to twist sts.

Rnd 1: *K2, p3tog, rep from * to end of rnd—99 sts.

Rnd 2: *K2, yo, k1, yo, rep from * to end of rnd—165 sts.

Rnds 3–9: Rep rnds 1 and 2 three more times, then work rnd 1 once more—99 sts.

Rnd 10: Switch to larger needles and knit.

pattern band 1 (daisy stitch)

Rnd 11: *Work (k2tog tbl, yo, k2tog tbl) into next 2 sts, k1* repeat from * to end of rnd—132 sts.

Rnd 12 & all even-numbered rnds: Knit.

Rnd 13: Move marker 1 st to left, then *k1, work (k3tog tbl, yo, k3tog tbl into next 3 sts),* rep from * to end of rnd.

Rnd 15: Move marker 2 sts to left, then *k1, work (k3togtbl, yo, k3togtbl) into next 3 sts,* rep from * to end of rnd.

Rnds 17–18: repeat Rnds 13–14—132 sts.

pattern band 2

Rnds 19–38: Work one full repeat of Chart 1, repeating chart 33 times each rnd.

pattern band 3

Rnds 39–66: Work one full repeat of Chart 2, repeating chart 33 times each rnd.

pattern band 4

Rnds 67–87: Work one full repeat of Chart 3, repeating chart 33 times each rnd.

BO all sts loosely.

FINISHING

Block piece to measurements, pinning out points and hem. Weave in all ends.

Mozzetta Capelet Chart 1

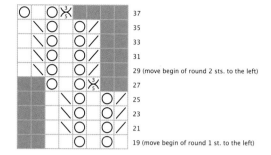

37
35
33
31
29 (move begin of round 2 sts. to the left)
27
25
23
21
19 (move begin of round 1 st. to the left)

Mozzetta Capelet Chart 2

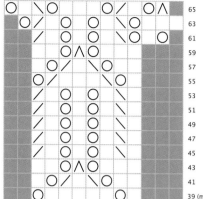

65
63
61
59
57
55
53
51
49
47
45
43
41
39 (move begin of round 1 st. to the left)

Mozzetta Capelet Chart 3

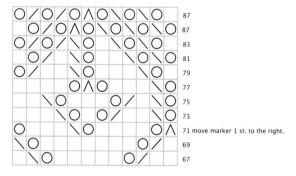

87
87
83
81
79
77
75
73
71 move marker 1 st. to the right.
69
67

☐	RS: knit / WS: purl
⊙	yo
╱	RS: k2tog / WS: p2tog
╲	RS: ssk / WS: p2tog tbl
▨	gray no stitch
⨯₅³	5 into 3 gathered tbl
⋀	RS: sl1, k2tog, psso / WS: sl1 wyif, p2tog tbl, psso

Only odd-numbered rounds are charted;
all even-numbered rounds are knit around.

DeBauliver top

PURE SILK IN A VIBRANT COLOR calls for a dramatic garment, and DeBauliver offers drama on many levels. A multidirectional knit, this piece can be worn as a flowing cape or as a top fitted at the waist. Panels of lace insertions that are knit horizontally alternate with panels of stockinette that are knit vertically. Shaped by increasing the amount of stitches in each stockinette panel, the cape flows to a lavish edging topped off with deep scallops. The yarn overs worked at the beginning of every row on the edging are necessary to block the edge out to its full width. Details on working a yarn over at the beginning of the row are outlined in the techniques section (see Yarn Overs on pages 12–14). The multidirectional construction provides knit-in seams that add structure to the finished piece while minimizing the amount of finishing.

SKILL LEVEL

INTERMEDIATE

FINISHED MEASUREMENTS

Circumference at hem 104"/264cm
Length 25"/64cm

MATERIALS AND TOOLS

Hamilton Yarns Heaven's Hand
    Silke (100% silk; 3.5oz/100g =
    258yd/235m): 5 skeins, color
    #219—approx 1075yd/983m of DK
    weight yarn **(3)**

Knitting needles: 4mm (size 6 U.S.)
    24" and 47" circular needles or size
    to obtain gauge

Tapestry needle

Coilless safety pin

2 yd one-inch silk ribbon

Stitch markers

Tapestry needle

GAUGE

Over Chart 1, 25 sts/25 rows = 5 1/2"/14cm wide × 4"/10cm tall after blocking
Always take time to check your gauge.

Special Abbreviations

4 into 1 decrease: Slip 2 sts together knitwise, k2tog, pass the 2 slipped stitches over this stitch. 4 stitches decreased into 1 stitch.

PATTERN STITCHES

chart 1: (see page 31)

Row 1 (RS): K5, (yo, ssk) three times, yo, sk2p, (yo, k2tog) four times, yo, k3—25 sts.

Row 2 AND ALL WS ROWS: P22, sl 1 wyif three times.

Row 3: K6, (yo, ssk) three times, yo, sk2p, (yo, k2tog) three times, yo, k4.

Row 5: K7, (yo, ssk) twice, yo, sk2p, (yo, k2tog) three times, yo, k5.

Row 7: K5, k2tog, yo, k1, (yo, ssk) twice, yo, sk2p, (yo, k2tog) twice, yo, k1, yo, ssk, k3.

Row 9: K4, k2tog, yo, k3, yo, ssk, yo, sk2p, (yo, k2tog) twice, yo, k3, yo, ssk, k2.

Row 11: K3, k2tog, yo, k5, yo, ssk, yo, sk2p, yo, k2tog, yo, k5, yo, ssk, k1.

Row 12: P22, sl 1 wyif three times— 25 sts.

chart 2: (see page 31)

Row 1 (RS): K3, k2tog, yo, k4—9 sts.

Row 2 AND ALL WS ROWS: P8, p2tog.

Row 3: K2, k2tog, yo, k1, yo, ssk, k2.

Row 5: K1, k2tog, yo, k3, yo, ssk, k1.

Row 7: K1, (k2tog, yo, k2) twice.

Row 9: K3, yo, sk2p, yo, k3.

Row 10: P8, p2tog—9 sts.

chart 3: (see page 31)

Row 1 (RS): K11, k2tog, yo, k6—19 sts.

Row 2 AND ALL WS ROWS: P18, p2tog.

Row 3: K10, k2tog, yo, k7.

Row 5: K9, k2tog, yo, k8.

Row 7: K8, k2tog, yo, k1, yo, ssk, k6.

Row 9: K7, k2tog, yo, k3, yo, ssk, k5.

Row 11: K6, k2tog, yo, k4, yo, ssk, k5.

Row 13: K5, k2tog, yo, k3, k2tog, yo, k1, yo, ssk, k4.

Rows 15 & 17: K5, k2tog, yo, k2, k2tog, yo, k3, yo, ssk, k3.

Row 19: K5, k2tog, yo, k4, yo, sk2p, yo, k5.

Row 21: K7, yo, ssk, k10.

Row 23: K8, yo, ssk, k9.

Row 25: K9, yo, ssk, k8.

Row 27: K7, k2tog, yo, k1, yo, ssk, k7.

Row 29: K6, k2tog, yo, k3, yo, ssk, k6.

Row 31: As Row 11.

Row 33: K5, k2tog, yo, k1, yo, ssk, k3, yo, ssk, k4.

Rows 35 & 37: K4, k2tog, yo, k3, yo, ssk, k2, yo, ssk, k4.

Row 39: K6, yo, sk2p, yo, k4, yo, ssk, k4—19 sts.

chart 4: (see page 32)

Note: St count changes throughout pattern.

Row 1 (RS): K3, yo, ssk, k3, (k2tog, yo) twice, k1, yo, k1, ssk, k5, k2tog, k1, yo, k2tog, yo, k1, yo, ssk, yo, k2—32 sts.

Row 2 (WS): Yo, p2tog, p27, yo, p2tog twice.

Row 3: K3, yo, ssk, k2, (k2tog, yo) twice, k3, yo, k1, ssk, k3, k2tog, k1, yo, k2tog, yo, k1, (yo, ssk) twice, yo, k2—33 sts.

Row 4: Yo, p2tog, p28, yo, p2tog twice.

Row 5: K3, yo, ssk, k1, (k2tog, yo) twice, k5, yo, k1, ssk, k1, k2tog, k1, yo, k2tog, yo, k1, (yo, ssk) three times, yo, k2—34 sts.

Row 6: Yo, p2tog, p29, yo, p2tog twice.

Row 7: K3, yo, ssk, (k2tog, yo) twice, k7, yo, k1, sk2p, k1, yo, k2tog, yo, k1, (yo, ssk) four times, yo, k2—35 sts.

Row 8: Yo, p2tog, p30, yo, p2tog twice.

Row 9: K3, yo, ssk, k2, yo, ssk, yo, k1, ssk, k5, k2tog, k1, yo, k1, (yo, ssk) six times, yo, k2—36 sts.

Row 10: Yo, p2tog, p31, yo, p2tog twice.

Row 11: (K3, yo, ssk) twice, yo, k1, ssk, k3, k2tog, k1, yo, k3, (yo, ssk) six times, yo, k2—37 sts.

Row 12: Yo, p2tog, p32, yo, p2tog twice.

Row 13: K3, yo, ssk, k4, yo, ssk, yo,

k1, ssk, k1, k2tog, k1, yo, k5, (yo, ssk) six times, yo, k2—38 sts.

Row 14: Yo, p2tog, p33, yo, p2tog twice.

Row 15: K3, yo, ssk, k5, yo, ssk, yo, k1, sk2p, k1, yo, k7, (yo, ssk) six times, yo, k2—39 sts.

Row 16: Yo, p2tog, p34, yo, p2tog twice.

Row 17: K3, yo, ssk, k3, (k2tog, yo) twice, k1, yo, k1, ssk, k5, k2tog, k1, (yo, k2tog) seven times, k1—38 sts.

Row 18: As Row 14.

Row 19: K3, yo, ssk, k2, (k2tog, yo) twice, k3, yo, k1, ssk, k3, k2tog, k1, (yo, k2tog) seven times, k1—37 sts.

Row 20: As Row 12.

Row 21: K3, yo, ssk, k1, (k2tog, yo) twice, k5, yo, k1, ssk, k1, k2tog, k1, (yo, k2tog) seven times, k1—36 sts.

Row 22: As Row 10.

Row 23: K3, yo, ssk, (k2tog, yo) twice, k7, yo, k1, sk2p, k1, (yo, k2tog) seven times, k1—35 sts.

Row 24: As Row 8.

Row 25: K3, yo, ssk, k2, yo, ssk, yo, k1, ssk, k5, k2tog, (k1, yo) twice, sk2p, (yo, k2tog) five times, k1—34 sts.

Row 26: As Row 6.

Row 27: (K3, yo, ssk) twice, yo, k1, ssk, k3, k2tog, k1, yo, k3, yo, sk2p, (yo, k2tog) four times, k1—33 sts.

Row 28: As Row 4.

Row 29: K3, yo, ssk, k4, yo, ssk, yo, k1, ssk, k1, k2tog, k1, yo, k5, yo, sk2p, (yo, k2tog) three times, k1—32 sts.

Row 30: As Row 2.

Row 31: K3, yo, ssk, k5, yo, ssk, yo,

k1, sk2p, k1, yo, k7, yo, sk2p, (yo, k2tog) twice, k1—31 sts.

Row 32: Yo, p2tog, p26, yo, p2tog twice—30 sts.

Notes
DeBauliver is knit from the top down, beginning with the collar. The collar is knit side to side, and then the body is knit in tiers, alternating stockinette stitch with lace insertions. Stockinette stitch tiers are knit horizontally after picking up stitches along selvedge edge of previous tier; lace insertions are knit side to side by casting on additional stitches and joining last stitch of WS rows to previous tier.

INSTRUCTIONS

collar

CO 25 sts.

Set-up row (WS): P22, sl 3 purlwise. Note: The last 3 sts of every WS row are slipped purlwise to create attached I-cord edging. This shapes the collar so that the upper edge draws in at the shoulders and the lower edge is longer for the body.

Work Chart 1 a total of 12 times.

BO all sts loosely knitwise—do not fasten off last st or cut yarn.

Tier 1: Stockinette St
With RS facing and using working yarn and rem st from previous tier, pick up and knit 140 sts in selvedge edge of collar (Note: Pick up sts along edge opposite slipped-stitch I-cord)—141 sts.

Turn and beg with a WS row, work 8 rows of stockinette st. Do not turn.

Tier 2: Lace Insertion
With RS of work still facing and using a knitted cast on, CO 9 sts. Turn.

Set-up row (WS): P8, purl 1st cast-on st tog with last st from previous (St st) tier. Turn.

Row 1 (RS): Work Row 1 of Chart 2 over 9 sts—turn.

Row 2: P8, purl next st tog with next st from previous (St st) section. Turn.

Cont in this manner, working successive rows of Chart 2 over 9 sts, joining last st tog with next st from previous section on WS rows, until you have completed 28 full repeats of Chart 2.

BO all sts loosely knitwise; do not fasten off last st or cut yarn.

Tier 3: Stockinette St
With RS facing, pick up and knit 280 sts across selvedge edge of previous (lace) tier—281 sts.

Beg with a WS row, work 14 rows of stockinette st. Do not turn.

Tier 4: Lace Insertion
With RS of work still facing, CO 19 sts. Turn.

Set-up row (WS): P18, purl next st tog with next st from previous (St st) section. Turn.

Row 1 (RS): Work Row 1 of Chart 3 over 19 sts—turn.

Row 2 (WS): P18, purl next st tog with next st from previous (St st) section. Turn.

Cont in this manner, working successive rows of Chart 3 over 19 sts, joining last st tog with next st from previous section on WS rows, until you have completed 14 full repeats of Chart 3.

BO all sts loosely knitwise; do not fasten off last st or cut yarn.

Tier 5: Stockinette St
With RS facing, pick up and knit 320 (approx 4 sts every 7 rows) sts across selvedge edge of previous (lace) tier—321 sts.

Beg with a WS row, work 14 rows of stockinette st. Do not turn.

leaf edging

CO 31 sts. Turn.

Set-up row (WS): P30, purl next st tog with next st from previous (St st) section. Turn.

Work Leaf Edging Chart over 31 sts only, joining last st of edging tog with next st from previous section on WS rows, until you have completed 20 full repeats of chart.

BO all sts loosely knitwise. Fasten off last st and break yarn.

FINISHING

Sew center back seam. Mark center front with coilless safety pin.

Weave in all ends and block as desired.

Beg at center front, with ribbon starting at RS of cape, weave ribbon through eyelet edging for 9"/23cm along right front, ending with ribbon on WS of cape. Skip the next 20"/51cm, then weave through the next 18"/46cm, ending with ribbon on WS of cape, skip the next 20"/51cm, weave through rem 9"/23cm, ending at center front with ribbon on RS of cape.

DeBauliver Top Chart 1

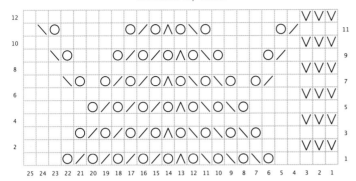

DeBauliver Top Chart 2

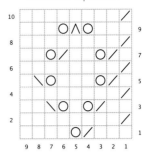

DeBauliver Top Chart 3

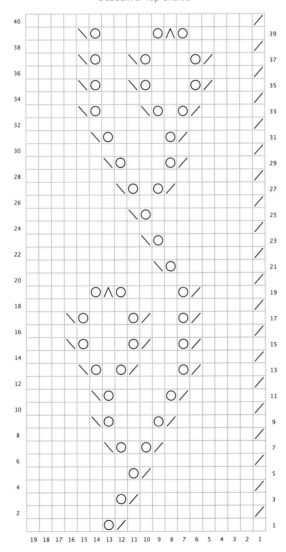

☐	RS: knit WS: purl
◯	yo
╱	RS: k2tog WS: p2tog
⋀	RS: sl1, k2tog, psso WS: sl1 wyif, p2tog tbl, psso
╲	RS: ssk WS: p2tog tbl
⋁	RS: slip WS: slip purlwise with yarn in front
▨	gray no stitch

All rows are charted

DeBauliver Top Chart 4

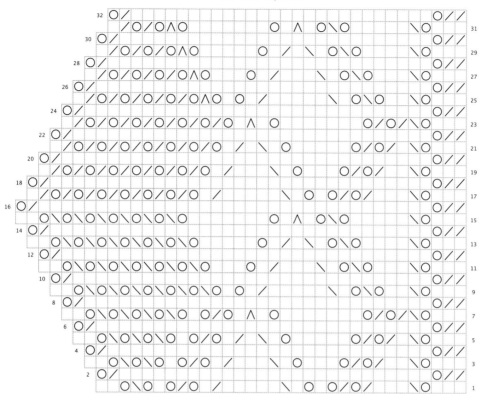

DeBauliver Schematic

All rows are charted

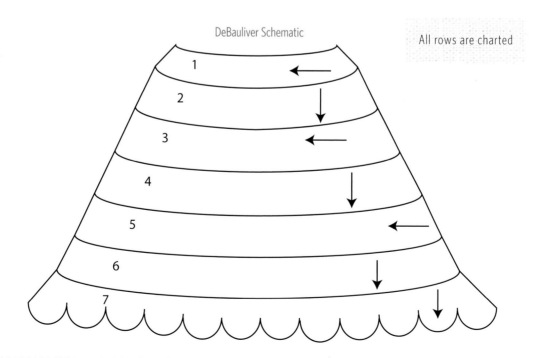

whorl shawl

A TYPICAL TOP-DOWN TRIANGLE SHAWL such as Arbor is created by combining two right triangles. We can make all kinds of fun shapes by playing around with the angles of the triangles as well as the number of triangles in the shawl. Whorl is made with five triangles that "explode" by increasing on every row, producing a fun swirly shawl that also can be worn as a capelet. The stitch pattern is a great introduction to patternig on both sides. It's a simple repeat that requires only k2tog on right-side rows and p2tog on wrong-side rows. The Whorl Gauntlets (page 41) are a great way to work your gauge swatch and practice the stitch motif without the shaping.

SKILL LEVEL

INTERMEDIATE

FINISHED MEASUREMENTS

Approx 38"/97cm at top edge
Approx 16"/41cm depth

MATERIALS AND TOOLS

Fiesta Yarns Katy (70% baby alpaca, 30% silk; 4oz/113g = 495yd/453m): 2 skeins, color peacock—approx 650yd/594m of Fingering weight yarn (1)

Knitting needles: 3.25mm (size 3 U.S.) 40" circular needles or size to obtain gauge

Stitch markers

Tapestry needle

GAUGE

1 repeat of highlighted sts on Chart 2 (8 sts/14 rows) = 1.5"/4cm × 3"/8cm after blocking
Always take time to check your gauge.

Notes

Shawl is worked from the top down, beginning with St st tab. Edge stitches are set off by markers and maintained in St st; work lace pattern over five center sections, which are separated by markers. Be careful to keep yarn overs on the correct sides of markers.

PATTERN STITCHES

chart 1: (see page 37)

Row 1 (RS): K2, yo, k5, k2tog, k1, yo—11 sts.

Row 2 (WS): Yo, p2, p2tog, p4, yo, p3—12 sts.

Row 3: K4, yo, k3, k2tog, k3, yo—13 sts.

Row 4: Yo, p4, p2tog, p2, yo, p5—14 sts.

Row 5: K6, yo, k1, k2tog, k5, yo—15 sts.

Row 6: Yo, p6, p2tog, yo, p7—16 sts.

chart 2: (see page 37)

Row 1 (RS): K1, *k6, k2tog, yo, rep from * as needed to last 7 sts, k7, yo—1 st incr.

Row 2 (WS): Yo, p1, yo, p7, *yo, p1, p2tog, p5, rep from * as needed to last st, p1—2 sts incr.

Row 3: K1, *k4, k2tog, k2, yo, rep from * as needed to last 10 sts, k4, k2tog, (k2, yo) twice—1 st incr.

Row 4: (Yo, p3) twice, p2tog, p3, *yo, p3, p2tog, p3, rep from * as needed to last st, p1—1 st incr.

Row 5: K1, *k2, k2tog, k4, yo, rep from * as needed to last 12 sts, k2, k2tog, (k4, yo) twice—1 st incr.

Row 6: (Yo, p5) twice, p2tog, p1, *yo, p5, p2tog, p1, rep from * as needed to last st, p1—1 st incr.

Row 7: K1, *k2tog, k6, yo, rep from * as needed to last 14 sts, k2tog, (k6, yo) twice—1 st incr.

Row 8: Yo, p6, yo, p2tog, p6, yo, *p2tog, p6, yo, rep from * as needed to last 2 sts, p2tog—1 st incr.

Row 9: K1, *k1, yo, k5, k2tog, rep from * as needed to last 16 sts, k1, yo, k5, k2tog, k1, yo, k7, yo—2 sts incr.

Row 10: (Yo, p2, p2tog, p4) twice, yo, p2, *p2tog, p4, yo, p2, rep from * as needed to last st, p1—1 st incr.

Row 11: K1, *k3, yo, k3, k2tog, rep from * as needed to last 19 sts, (k3, yo, k3, k2tog) twice, k3, yo—1 st incr.

Row 12: (Yo, p4, p2tog, p2) twice, yo, p4, *p2tog, p2, yo, p4, rep from * as needed to last st, p1—1 st incr.

Row 13: K1, *k5, yo, k1, k2tog, rep from * as needed to last 21 sts, (k5, yo, k1, k2tog) twice, k5, yo—1 st incr.

Row 14: (Yo, p6, p2tog) twice, yo, p6, *p2tog, yo, p6, rep from * as needed to last st, p1—1 st incr.

INSTRUCTIONS

CO 3 sts.

Beg with a RS row, work in St st for 66 rows.

NEXT (RS) ROW: K3, pick up and knit 49 sts in left selvedge edge, pick up and knit 3 sts in cast-on edge—55 sts.

NEXT (WS) row: P3, PM, [p10, PM] five times, p2. You have divided your knitting into five sections with a selvedge edge on either side; note that the selvedge consists of 2 sts at the beginning of the RS and 3 sts at the end.

Begin working Chart 1 lace pattern as follows:

Row 1 (RS): K2, sm, *work Row 1 of Chart 1 to next m, sm, rep from * four more times, k3—60 sts.

Row 2 (WS): P3, sm, *work Row 2 of Chart 1 to next m, sm, rep from * four more times, p2—65 sts.

Rows 3–6: Cont in this fashion, working 1st two and last three sts in St st, and rep each successive row of chart five times per row (once in each of five sections)—85 sts after Row 6.

Begin working Chart 2 lace pattern as follows:

NEXT ROW (RS): K2, sm, *work Row 1 of Chart 2 to m, sm, rep from * four more times, k3—90 sts.

Row 2: P3, sm, *work Row 2 of Chart 2 to next m, sm, rep from* four more times, p2—100 sts.

Rows 3–14: Cont in this fashion, working 1st two and last three sts in St st, and rep each successive row of Chart 2 five times per row (once in each of five sections)—165 sts after first full repeat of Chart 2.

Cont working patt as established, working six more full repeats of Chart 2, adding repeats as needed as sts incr—645 sts after last full repeat of Chart 2.

Row 105: BO all sts loosely knitwise.

FINISHING

Weave in all ends and block.

Whorl Shawl Chart 1

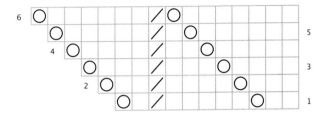

Whorl Shawl Chart 2

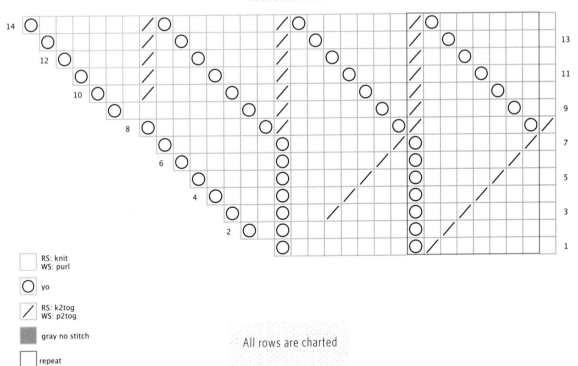

	RS: knit / WS: purl
O	yo
/	RS: k2tog / WS: p2tog
▨	gray no stitch
	repeat

All rows are charted

aria gauntlets

Simple construction, minimal finishing, and a show-stopping lace motif come together to create these gauntlets, which are perfect for a night at the opera or a day in the park. The pieces are knit flat and then seamed together at the selvedges, leaving an opening for the thumb. You can make them short, as photographed here, or repeat the chart more times for elegant elbow-length sleeves. This "recipe"—creating an 8-inch-wide rectangle—is a great way to make your swatches do double duty. You can make gauntlets out of any of the stitch patterns in the book by using a little math.

SKILL LEVEL

EASY

FINISHED MEASUREMENTS

Circumference approx 8"/20cm
Length approx 10"/25cm

MATERIALS AND TOOLS

Lotus Yarns Autumn Wind (90% cotton, 10% cashmere; 50g = 175yd/160m): 1 skein, color purple #22—approx 153yd/140m of sport weight yarn **(2)**

Knitting needles: 2.75mm (size 2 U.S.) or size to obtain gauge

GAUGE

1 repeat of Chart 1 (40 sts/20 rows) = 8"/20cm wide × 2½"/6cm tall after blocking
Always take time to check your gauge.

Notes

Gauntlets are knit as a rectangle, blocked, and then sewn together, leaving an opening at the seam for the thumb. Use Chart 1 for right gauntlet and Chart 2 for left gauntlet. Only RS rows are charted; all WS rows are purled.

PATTERN STITCHES

Picot cast on: Using knitted cast on, *CO 4 sts, BO 2 sts, sl rem st onto left needle, rep from * until required number of sts is cast on.

Picot bind off: BO 2 sts knitwise, *sl rem st onto left needle and CO 2 sts, BO 4 sts kwise, rep from * until all sts are bound off, then fasten off last st.

right gauntlet (chart 1): (see page 42)

Row 1 (RS): K5, yo, sk2p, yo, k3, (k2tog, yo) twice, k1, (yo, ssk) twice, k3, yo, sk2p, yo, (k3, yo, sk2p, yo) twice, k2.

Row 2 and all WS rows: Purl.

Row 3: K2, yo, sk2p, yo, k3, yo, ssk, (k2tog, yo, k1) twice, yo, ssk, k1, yo, ssk, k2tog, yo, k3, (yo, sk2p, yo, k3) twice, k2.

Row 5: K5, yo, sk2p, yo, k1, k2tog, yo, k2, k2tog, yo, k1, yo, ssk, k2, yo, ssk, k1, yo, sk2p, yo, (k3, yo, sk2p, yo) twice, k2.

Row 7: K2, yo, sk2p, yo, k3, yo, sk2p, yo, k2, k2tog, yo, k1, yo, ssk, k2, yo, sk2p, yo, k3, (yo, sk2p, yo, k3) twice, k2.

Row 9: K5, yo, sk2p, yo, k1, yo, ssk, k9, k2tog, yo, k1, yo, sk2p, yo, (k3, yo, sk2p, yo) twice, k2.

Row 11: K2, yo, sk2p, yo, k3, (yo, ssk) twice, k7, (k2tog, yo) twice, k3, (yo, sk2p, yo, k3) twice, k2.

Row 13: K5, yo, sk2p, yo, k3, yo, ssk, k5, k2tog, yo, k3, yo, sk2p, yo, (k3, yo, sk2p, yo) twice, k2.

Row 15: K2, yo, sk2p, yo, k3, yo, sk2p, yo, k1, yo, ssk, k3, k2tog, yo, k1, yo, sk2p, yo, k3, (yo, sk2p, yo, k3) twice, k2.

Row 17: K5, yo, sk2p, yo, k3, (yo, ssk) twice, k1, (k2tog, yo) twice, k3, yo, sk2p, yo, (k3, yo, sk2p, yo) twice, k2.

Row 19: K2, (yo, sk2p, yo, k3) six times, k2.

Row 20: Purl.

left gauntlet (chart 2): (see page 42)

Row 1 (RS): K2, (yo, sk2p, yo, k3) twice, yo, sk2p, yo, k3, (k2tog, yo) twice, k1, (yo, ssk) twice, k3, yo, sk2p, yo, k5.

Row 2 and all WS rows: Purl.

Row 3: K2, (k3, yo, sk2p, yo) twice, k3, yo, ssk, (k2tog, yo, k1) twice, yo, ssk, k1, yo, ssk, k2tog, yo, k3, yo, sk2p, yo, k2.

Row 5: K2, (yo, sk2p, yo, k3) twice, yo, sk2p, yo, k1, k2tog, yo, k2, k2tog, yo, k1, yo, ssk, k2, yo, ssk, k1, yo, sk2p, yo, k5.

Row 7: K2, (k3, yo, sk2p, yo) three times, yo, k2, k2tog, yo, k1, yo, ssk, k2, yo, sk2p, yo, k3, yo, sk2p, yo, k2.

Row 9: K2, (yo, sk2p, yo, k3) twice, yo, sk2p, yo, k1, yo, ssk, k9, k2tog, yo, k1, yo, sk2p, yo, k5.

Row 11: K2, (k3, yo, sk2p, yo) twice, k3, (yo, ssk) twice, k7, (k2tog, yo) twice, k3, yo, sk2p, yo, k2.

Row 13: K2, (yo, sk2p, yo, k3) twice, yo, sk2p, yo, k3, yo, ssk, k5, k2tog, yo, k3, yo, sk2p, yo, k5.

Row 15: K2, (k3, yo, sk2p, yo) three times, k1, yo, ssk, k3, k2tog, yo, k1, yo, sk2p, yo, k3, yo, sk2p, yo, k2.

Row 17: K2, (yo, sk2p, yo, k3) three times, (yo, ssk) twice, k1, (k2tog, yo) twice, k3, yo, sk2p, yo, k5.

Row 19: K2, (k3, yo, sk2p, yo) six times, k2.

Row 20: Purl.

INSTRUCTIONS

right gauntlet

Using the picot cast on, CO 40 sts.

Beginning with a RS row, work 2 rows in St st.

Work Chart 1, repeating highlighted sts twice across each row, until you have completed four full repeats of Chart 1 (80 rows completed).

BO all sts using the picot bind off. Cut yarn, leaving 16"/20cm tail for seaming.

left gauntlet

Using the picot cast on, CO 40 sts.

Beginning with a RS row, work 2 rows in St st.

Work Chart 2, repeating highlighted sts twice across each row, until you have completd four full repeats of Chart 2 (80 rows completed).

BO all sts using the picot bind off. Cut yarn, leaving 16"/20cm tail for seaming.

FINISHING

Block pieces to measurements. Beginning at bound-off edge, seam long edges of gauntlet together for 6"/15cm; leave the next 2½"/6cm open for thumb hole; seam the remaining 1"/2.5cm to cast-on edge. Repeat for other gauntlet. Weave in all ends.

whorl gauntlets

Cast on 44 sts.

Row 1 (WS): p2, pm, p40, pm, p2

Begin working Chart 2 lace pattern, repeating the highlighted sts only of Chart 2 five times between the markers, keeping the 1st and last 2 sts of every row in stockinette stitch.

Work Chart rows 1–14 until gauntlets are desired length. Bind off loosely, block, and seam as for aria gauntlets.

montauk gauntlets

Cast on 23 sts.

Row 1 (WS) p2, pm, p19, pm, p2

Begin working Chart 4 between the markers, keeping the 1st and last 2 sts of every row in stockinette stitch.

Work chart rows 1–10 until gauntlets are desired length. Bind off loosely, block, and seam as for aria gauntlets.

Aria Gauntlets Chart 1

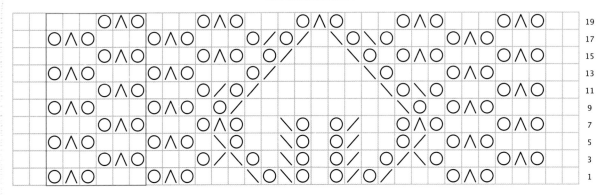

Aria Gauntlets Chart 2

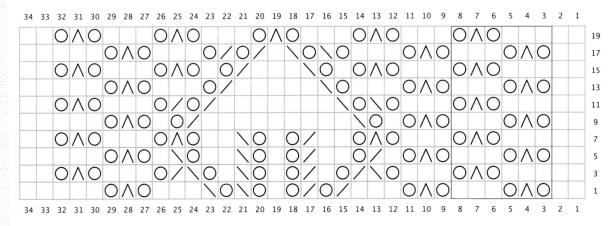

Only odd-numbered rows are charted;
all even-numbered rows are purl across.

	RS: knit WS: purl
O	yo
∧	RS: sl1, k2tog, psso WS: sl1 wyif, p2tog tbl, psso
/	RS: k2tog WS: p2tog
\	RS: ssk WS: p2tog tbl
	repeat

Aria Gauntlets Schematic

Bind Off

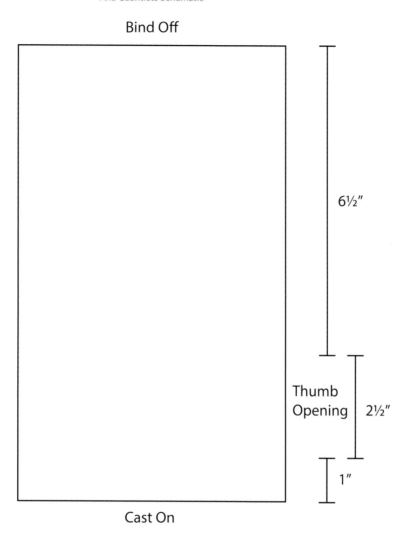

6½"

Thumb
Opening   2½"

1"

Cast On

triangles

MY FAVORITE SHAPE to design with is the triangle. Once you get the trick of the standard top-down triangle shawl shaping, as in Arbor, you can translate it to a variety of garments, including a raglan sweater, assorted circular garments and accessories (such as Peony), and even capes. In this section I also explore another way of shaping a triangle in Amaryllis.

 *arbor triangular shawl*

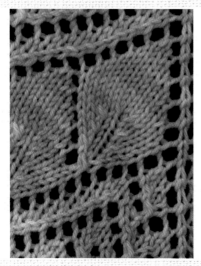

A **CLASSIC TOP-DOWN TRIANGLE KNIT** in worsted weight wool, Arbor is a great project to start your exploration of lace knitting. The lace motif is actually a bias (diagonal) motif mirrored on each side of the center spine—an excellent visual explanation of the way the triangles are shaped.

You can work several variations of this shawl by simply altering the order of the charts worked. Working the charts exactly as called for in the pattern creates a shawl with horizontal bands of the lace motif. If, however, you reverse the order of the charts in each section (for example, working Chart 2 in the first section, Chart 1 in the second section, and so on), the resulting shawl will have vertical bands of lace. Or you can create an asymmetric look by working only the even-numbered charts in each section throughout the shawl.

SKILL LEVEL

EASY

FINISHED MEASUREMENTS

Width (across wingspan) 57"/145cm
Height 32"/81cm

MATERIALS AND TOOLS

Hamilton Yarns Heaven's Hand Wool
  Classic (100% wool; 3.5oz/100g
  = 219yd/200m): 3 skeins, color
  lime—approx 500yd/457m of
  worsted weight yarn (4)

Knitting needles: 5mm (size 8 U.S.)
  32" circular needles or size to
  obtain gauge

Stitch markers

Tapestry needle

GAUGE

1 repeat of highlighted section in Chart 3 (36 sts/36 RS) = 8"/20cm wide ×
6"/15cm tall after blocking
Always take time to check your gauge.

Notes

Shawl is knit from the top down. Begin with a stockinette stitch tab, into which you will pick up stitches for a 3-stitch stockinette stitch border and the shawl body. Increases are worked at the beginning and end and on each side of the center spine on each right-side row.

Only odd-numbered rows are charted, all even-numbered rows are purl across.

PATTERN STITCHES

arbor triangular shawl chart 1: (see page 52)

Row 1 (RS): Yo, k2, yo.

Row 2 AND ALL WS ROWS: P.

Row 3: Yo, k4, yo.

Row 5: Yo, k1, k2tog, yo, k3, yo.

Row 7: Yo, k1, yo, ssk, k1, k2tog, yo, k2, yo.

Row 9: Yo, k3, yo, sk2p, yo, k4, yo.

Row 11: (Yo, k1, k2tog) three times, yo, k3, yo.

Row 13: (Yo, k1, yo, ssk, k1, k2tog) twice, yo, k2, yo.

Row 15: (Yo, k3, yo, sk2p) twice, yo, k4, yo.

Row 17: (Yo, k1, k2tog) five times, yo, k3, yo.

Row 19: (Yo, k1, yo, ssk, k1, k2tog) three times, yo, k2, yo.

Row 21: (Yo, k3, yo, sk2p) three times, yo, k1, k2tog, yo, k1, yo.

Row 23: (Yo, k1, k2tog) seven times, yo, k3, yo.

Row 25: (Yo, k1, yo, ssk, k1, k2tog) three times, yo, k1, k2tog, yo, k5, yo.

Row 27: (Yo, k3, yo, sk2p) three times, yo, k1, k2tog, yo, k7, yo.

Row 29: (Yo, k1, k2tog) seven times, yo, k9, yo.

Row 31: (Yo, k1, yo, ssk, k1, k2tog) three times, yo, k1, k2tog, yo, k11, yo.

Row 33: (Yo, k3, yo, sk2p) three times, yo, k1, k2tog, yo, k1, yo, k3, ssk, k1, k2tog, k3, yo, k1, yo.

Row 35: (Yo, k1, k2tog) seven times, yo, k3, yo, k2, ssk, k1, k2tog, k2, yo, k3, yo.

Row 36: P.

arbor triangular shawl chart 2: (see page 52)

Row 1 (RS): Yo, k2, yo.

Row 2 and all WS rows: P.

Row 3: Yo, k4, yo.

Row 5: Yo, k3, yo, ssk, k1, yo.

Row 7: Yo, k2, yo, ssk, k1, k2tog, yo, k1, yo.

Row 9: Yo, k4, yo, sk2p, yo, k3, yo.

Row 11: Yo, k3, (yo, ssk, k1) three times, yo.

Row 13: Yo, k2, (yo, ssk, k1, k2tog, yo, k1) two times, yo.

Row 15: Yo, k4, (yo, sk2p, yo, k3) twice, yo.

Row 17: Yo, k3, (yo, ssk, k1) five times, yo.

Row 19: Yo, k2, (yo, ssk, k1, k2tog, yo, k1) three times, yo.

Row 21: Yo, k1, yo, ssk, k1, (yo, sk2p, yo, k3) three times, yo.

Row 23: Yo, k3, (yo, ssk, k1) seven times, yo.

Row 25: Yo, k5, yo, ssk, (k1, yo, ssk, k1, k2tog, yo) three times, k1, yo.

Row 27: Yo, k7, yo, ssk, k1, (yo, sk2p, yo, k3) three times, yo.

Row 29: Yo, k9, (yo, ssk, k1) seven times, yo.

Row 31: Yo, k11, yo, ssk, (k1, yo, ssk, k1, k2tog, yo) three times, k1, yo.

Row 33: Yo, k1, yo, k3, ssk, k1, k2tog, k3, yo, k1, yo, ssk, k1, (yo, sk2p, yo, k3) three times.

Row 35: Yo, k3, yo, k2, ssk, k1, k2tog, k2, yo, k3, (yo, ssk, k1) seven times, yo.

Row 36: P.

arbor triangular shawl chart 3: (see page 52)

Row 37 (RS): [(Yo, k1 yo, ssk, k1, k2tog) three times, yo, k1, k2tog, yo, k5, yo, k1, ssk, k1, k2tog, k1, yo, k1, k2tog,] yo, k2, yo.

Row 38 and all WS rows: P.

Row 39: [(Yo, k3, yo, sk2p) three times, yo, k1, k2tog, yo, k7, yo, ssk, k1, k2tog, yo, k1, k2tog,] yo, k4, yo.

Row 41: [(Yo, k1, k2tog) seven times, yo, k9, yo, sk2p, yo, k1, k2tog,] yo, k1, k2tog, yo, k3, yo.

Row 43: [(Yo, k1, yo, ssk, k1, k2tog) three times, yo, k1, k2tog, yo, k6, k2tog, k4, yo, k1, k2tog,] yo, k1, yo, ssk, k1, k2tog, yo, k2, yo.

Row 45: [(Yo, k3, yo, sk2p) three times, yo, k1, k2tog, yo, k1, yo, k3, ssk, k1, k2tog, k3, yo, k1, k2tog,] yo, k3, yo, sk2p, yo, k4, yo.

Row 47: [(Yo, k1, k2tog) seven times, yo, k3, yo, k2, ssk, k1, k2tog, k2, yo, k1, k2tog,] (yo, k1, k2tog) three times, yo, k3, yo.

Row 49: [(Yo, k1, yo, ssk, k1, k2tog) three times, yo, k1, k2tog, yo, k5, yo, k1, ssk, k1, k2tog, k1, yo, k1, k2tog,] (yo, k1, yo, ssk, k1, k2tog) twice, yo, k2, yo.

Row 51: [(Yo, k3, yo, sk2p) three times, yo, k1, k2tog, yo, k7, yo, ssk, k1, k2tog, yo, k1, k2tog,] (yo, k3, yo, sk2p) twice, yo, k4, yo.

Row 53: [(Yo, k1, k2tog) seven times, yo, k9, yo, sk2p, yo, k1, k2tog,] (yo, k1, k2tog) five times, yo, k3, yo.

Row 55: [(Yo, k1, yo, ssk, k1, k2tog) three times, yo, k1, k2tog, yo, k6, k2tog, k4, yo, k1, k2tog,] (yo, k1, yo, ssk, k1, k2tog) three times, yo, k2, yo.

Row 57: [(Yo, k3, yo, sk2p) three times, yo, k1, k2tog, yo, k1, yo, k3, ssk, k1, k2tog, k3, yo, k1, k2tog,] (yo, k3, yo, sk2p) three times, yo, k1, k2tog, yo, k1, yo.

Row 59: [(Yo, k1, k2tog) seven times, yo, k3, yo, k2, ssk, k1, k2tog, k2, yo, k1, k2tog,] (yo, k1, k2tog) seven times, yo, k3, yo.

Row 61: [(Yo, k1, yo, ssk, k1, k2tog) three times, yo, k1, k2tog, yo, k5, yo, k1, ssk, k1, k2tog, k1, yo, k1, k2tog,] (yo, k1, yo, ssk, k1, k2tog) three times, yo, k1, k2tog, yo, k5, yo.

Row 63: [Yo, (k3, yo, sk2p, yo) three times, k1, k2tog, yo, k7, yo, ssk, k1, k2tog, yo, k1, k2tog,] (yo, k3, yo, sk2p) three times, yo, k1, k2tog, yo, k7, yo.

Row 65: [(Yo, k1, k2tog) seven times, yo, k9, yo, sk2p, yo, k1, k2tog,] (yo, k1, k2tog) seven times, yo, k9, yo.

Row 67: [(Yo, k1, yo, ssk, k1, k2tog) three times, yo, k1, k2tog, yo, k6, k2tog, k4, yo, k1, k2tog,] yo, k1, (yo, ssk, k1, k2tog, yo, k1) three times, k2tog, yo, k11, yo.

Row 69: [(Yo, k3, yo, sk2p) three times, yo, k1, k2tog, yo, k1, yo, k3, ssk, k1, k2tog, k3, yo, k1, k2tog,] yo, k3, (yo, sk2p, yo, k3) twice, yo, sk2p, yo, k1, k2tog, yo, k1, yo, k3, ssk, k1, k2tog, k3, yo, k1, yo.

Row 71: [(Yo, k1, k2tog) seven times, yo, k3, yo, k2, ssk, k1, k2tog, k2, yo, k1, k2tog,] yo, k1, (k2tog, yo, k1) six times, k2tog, yo, k3, yo, k2, ssk, k1, k2tog, k2, yo, k3, yo.

Row 72: P.

arbor triangular shawl chart 4: (see page 53)

Row 37 (RS): Yo, k2, yo, [ssk, k1, yo, k1, ssk, k1, k2tog, k1, yo, k5, yo, ssk, (k1, yo, ssk, k1, k2tog, yo) three times, k1, yo.]

Row 38 and all WS rows: P.

Row 39: Yo, k4, yo, [ssk, k1, yo, ssk, k1, k2tog, yo, k7, yo, ssk, k1, (yo, sk2p, yo, k3) ×3, yo.]

Row 41: Yo, k3, yo, ssk, k1, yo, [ssk, k1, yo, sk2p, yo, k9, (yo, ssk, k1) seven times, yo.]

Row 43: Yo, k2, yo, ssk, k1, k2tog, yo, k1, yo, [ssk, k1, yo, k4, ssk, k6, yo, ssk, (k1, yo, ssk, k1, k2tog, yo) three times, k1, yo.]

Row 45: Yo, k4, yo, sk2p, yo, k3, yo, [ssk, k1, yo, k3, ssk, k1, k2tog, k3, yo, k1, yo, ssk, k1, (yo, sk2p, yo, k3) three times, yo.]

Row 47: Yo, k3, (yo, ssk, k1) three times, yo, [ssk, k1, yo, k2, ssk, k1,

k2tog, k2, yo, k3, (yo, ssk, k1) seven times, yo.]

Row 49: Yo, k2, (yo, ssk, k1, k2tog, yo, k1) twice, yo, [ssk, k1, yo, k1, ssk, k1, k2tog, k1, yo, k5, yo, ssk, (k1, yo, ssk, k1, k2tog, yo) three times, k1, yo.]

Row 51: Yo, k4, (yo, sk2p, yo, k3) twice, yo, [ssk, k1, yo, ssk, k1, k2tog, yo, k7, yo, ssk, k1, (yo, sk2p, yo, k3) three times, yo.]

Row 53: Yo, k3, (yo, ssk, k1) five times, yo, [ssk, k1, yo, sk2p, yo, k9, (yo, ssk, k1) seven times, yo.]

Row 55: Yo, k2, (yo, ssk, k1, k2tog, yo, k1) three times, yo, [ssk, k1, yo, k4, ssk, k6, yo, ssk, (k1, yo, ssk, k1, k2tog, yo) three times, k1, yo.]

Row 57: Yo, k1, yo, ssk, k1, (yo, sk2p, yo, k3) three times, yo, [ssk, k1, yo, k3, ssk, k1, k2tog, k3, yo, k1, yo, ssk, k1, (yo, sk2p, yo, k3) three times, yo.]

Row 59: Yo, k3, (yo, ssk, k1) seven times, yo, [ssk, k1, yo, k2, ssk, k1, k2tog, k2, yo, k3, (yo, ssk, k1) seven times, yo.]

Row 61: Yo, k5, yo, ssk, (k1, yo, ssk, k1, k2tog, yo) three times, k1, yo, [ssk, k1, yo, k1, ssk, k1, k2tog, k1, yo, k5, yo, ssk, (k1, yo, ssk, k1, k2tog, yo) three times, k1, yo.]

Row 63: Yo, k7, yo, ssk, k1, (yo, sk2p, yo, k3) three times, yo, [ssk, k1, yo, ssk, k1, k2tog, yo, k7, yo, ssk, k1, (yo, sk2p, yo, k3) three times, yo.]

Row 65: Yo, k9, (yo, ssk, k1) seven times, yo, [ssk, k1, yo, sk2p, yo, k9, (yo, ssk, k1) seven times, yo.]

Row 67: Yo, k11, yo, ssk, (k1, yo, ssk, k1, k2tog, yo) three times, k1, yo, [ssk, k1, yo, k4, ssk, k6, yo, ssk, (k1, yo, ssk, k1, k2tog, yo) three times, k1, yo.]

Row 69: Yo, k1, yo, k3, ssk, k1, k2tog, k3, yo, k1, yo, ssk, k1, (yo, sk2p, yo,

k3) twice, yo, sk2p, yo, k3, yo, [ssk, k1, yo, k3, ssk, k1, k2tog, k3, yo, k1, yo, ssk, k1, (yo, sk2p, yo, k3) three times, yo.]

Row 71: Yo, k3, yo, k2, ssk, k1, k2tog, k2, yo, k3, (yo, ssk, k1) seven times, yo, [ssk, k1, yo, k2, ssk, k1, k2tog, k2, yo, k3, (yo, ssk, k1) seven times, yo.]

Row 72: P.

arbor triangular shawl chart 5: (see page 53)

Row 109 (RS): (Yo, k1, yo, ssk, k1, k2tog) three times, (yo, k1, k2tog) twice, yo, k2, yo, k1, ssk, k1, k2tog, k1, yo, k1, k2tog, yo, k2, yo.

Row 110 & all WS rows: P.

Row 111: (Yo, k3, yo, sk2p) three times, (yo, k1, k2tog) three times, yo, k1, yo, ssk, k1, k2tog, yo, k1, k2tog, yo, k1, k2tog, yo, k1, yo.

Row 113: (Yo, k1, k2tog) nine times, yo, k3, yo, sk2p, yo, k1, k2tog, yo, k1, k2tog, yo, k3, yo.

Row 115: Yo, k1, yo, ssk, k1, k2tog, yo, k1, yo, ssk, k1, k2tog, yo, k1, yo, ssk, (k1, k2tog, yo) six times, k1, k2tog, yo, k1, yo, ssk, k1, k2tog, yo, k2, yo.

Row 117: Yo, k3, yo, (sk2p, yo, k3, yo) twice, sk2p, (yo, k1, k2tog) six times, yo, k3, yo, sk2p, yo, k4, yo.

Row 118: P.

arbor triangular shawl chart 6: (see page 53)

Row 109 (RS): Yo, k2, yo, ssk, k1, yo, k1, ssk, k1, k2tog, k1, yo, k2, yo, ssk, k1, yo, ssk, (k1, yo, ssk, k1, k2tog, yo) three times, k1, yo.

Row 110 & all WS rows: P.

Row 111: Yo, (k1, yo, ssk) three times,

k1, k2tog, yo, (k1, yo, ssk) three times, k1, (yo, sk2p, yo, k3) three times, yo.

Row 113: Yo, k3, (yo, ssk, k1) twice, yo, sk2p, yo, k3, (yo, ssk, k1) nine times, yo.

Row 115: Yo, k2, yo, ssk, k1, k2tog, yo, k1, yo, (ssk, k1, yo) six times, (ssk, k1, k2tog, yo, k1, yo) twice, ssk, k1, k2tog, yo, k1, yo.

Row 117: Yo, k4, yo, sk2p, yo, k3, yo, (ssk, k1, yo) six times, (sk2p, yo, k3, yo) twice, sk2p, yo, k3, yo.

Row 118: P.

Notes

Shawl is knit from the top down. Begin with a stockinette stitch tab into which you will pick up stitches for a three-stitch stockinette stitch border and the shawl body. Slip all markers as you come to them, being careful to keep yarn overs on the correct side of stitch markers.

INSTRUCTIONS

CO 3 sts.

Beginning with a RS row, work 6 rows in St st.

Next row (RS): K3, do not turn, pick up 5 sts in selvedge, pick up 3 sts in cast-on edge—11 sts.

Set-up row (WS): P3, PM, p2, PM, p1, PM, p2, PM, p3.

Begin lace pattern

Row 1 and all RS rows: K3, work Chart 1 between markers, k1, work Chart 2 between markers, k3.

Row 2 and all WS rows: Purl.

Cont to work through Row 36 of Charts 1 and 2 as established, maintaining 1st and last 3 sts and center spine stitch in St st—83 sts.

Row 37 and all RS rows: K3, work Chart 3 between markers, k1, work Chart 4 between markers, k3.

Row 38 and all WS rows: Purl.

Cont to work through Row 72 of Charts 3 and 4 as established, maintaining 1st and last 3 sts and center spine st in St st—155 sts.

Rows 73–108: Work as Rows 37–73, working highlighted stitches on charts (or bracketed stitches in written-out pattern) twice between markers—227 sts.

Row 109 and all RS rows: K3, work Chart 5 between markers, k1, work Chart 6 between markers, k3.

Row 110 & all WS rows: Purl—247 sts.

Row 119: BO all sts loosely knitwise.

FINISHING

Weave in all ends. Block piece to measurements.

Arbor Triangular Shawl Chart 1

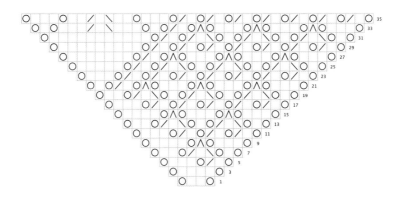

Arbor Triangular Shawl Chart 2

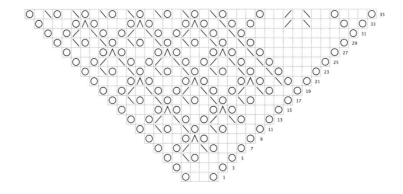

Arbor Triangular Shawl Chart 3

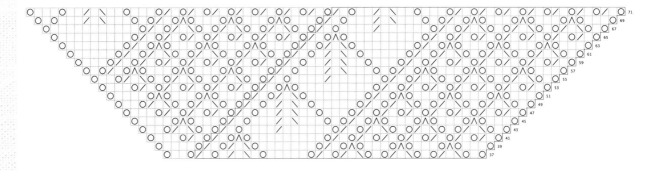

Arbor Triangular Shawl Chart 4

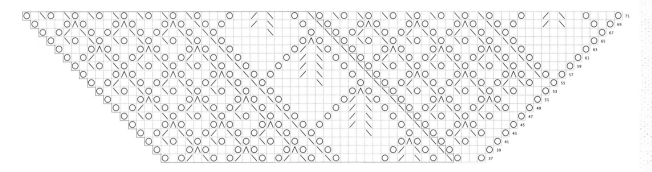

Arbor Triangular Shawl Chart 5

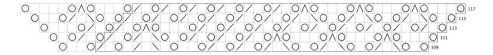

Arbor Triangular Shawl Chart 6

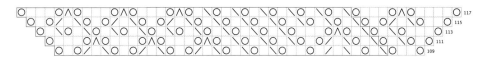

	RS: knit
	WS: purl

○	yo

	RS: ssk
\	WS: p2tog tbl

	RS: k2tog
/	WS: p2tog

	RS: sl1, k2tog, psso
∧	WS: sl1 wyif, p2tog tbl, psso

	gray no stitch

	repeat

Only odd-numbered rows are charted;
all even-numbered rows are purl across.

amaryllis entrelac shawl

AMARYLLIS IS A TRIANGLE SHAWL that is knit from the bottom up rather than by using traditional top-down construction. The entrelac diamonds are built from the lace edging and feature Estonian lace motifs rich with nupps. The self-striping yarn features a long repeat—a great combination with entrelac. If you haven't done much entrelac knitting, you may want to swatch a few tiers in plain stockinette stitch to get comfortable before tackling the lace.

SKILL LEVEL

⬤◼◻◼⬤

EXPERIENCED

FINISHED MEASUREMENTS

Approx 68" across top edge × 58" from point to top edge

MATERIALS AND TOOLS

Kauni Effektgarn (100% wool; 100g = 440yd/402m): 4 skeins, color EN—approx 1740yd/1591m of Fingering weight yarn ❶

Knitting needles: 4mm (size 6 U.S.) 42" circular needles or size to obtain gauge

GAUGE

1 repeat of Chart 2 (22 sts/44 rows) = 4 1/2"/11cm wide × 6"/15cm tall after blocking

Special Abbreviations

2/2: into next 2 sts, work (k2tog, k2tog tbl) nupp: see p. 13

PATTERN STITCHES

Amaryllis Entrelac Shawl Chart 1: (see page 60)

Row 1 (RS): K1, yo, k8, ssk, (k2tog, k8, yo, k2, yo, k8, ssk) nine times, k2tog, k8, yo, k1—440 sts.

Row 2 AND ALL WS ROWS: Purl.

Row 3: K2, yo, k7, ssk, (k2tog, k7, yo, k4, yo, k7, ssk) nine times, k2tog, k7, yo, k2.

Row 5: K1, yo, ssk, yo, k6, ssk, (k2tog, k6, yo, k2tog, yo, k2, yo, ssk, yo, k6, ssk) nine times, k2tog, k6, yo, k3.

Row 7: K2, yo, ssk, yo, k5, ssk, (k2tog, k5, yo, k2tog, yo, k4, yo, ssk, yo, k5, ssk) nine times, k2tog, k5, yo, k2tog, yo, k2.

Row 9: K3, yo, ssk, yo, k4, ssk, (k2tog, k4, yo, k2tog, yo, k2, nupp twice, k2, yo, ssk, yo, k4, ssk) nine times, k2tog, k4, yo, k2tog, yo, k3.

Row 11: K4, yo, ssk, yo, k3, ssk, (k2tog, k3, yo, k2tog, yo, k2, nupp, 2-2, nupp, k2, yo, ssk, yo, k3, ssk) nine times, k2tog, k3, yo, k2tog, yo, k4.

Row 13: K5, yo, ssk, yo, k2, ssk, (k2tog, k2, yo, k2tog, yo, k4, nupp twice, k4, yo, ssk, yo, k2, ssk) nine times, k2tog, k2, yo, k2tog, yo, k5.

Row 15: K6, yo, ssk, yo, k1, ssk, (k2tog, k1, yo, k2tog, yo, k12, yo, ssk, yo, k1, ssk) nine times, k2tog, k1, yo, k2tog, yo, k6.

Row 17: K7, (yo, ssk) twice, [(k2tog, yo) twice, k14, (yo, ssk) twice] nine times, (k2tog, yo) twice, k7.

Row 19: K8, yo, ssk, k1, (k1, k2tog, yo, k16, yo, ssk, k1) nine times, k1, k2tog, yo, k8.

Row 21: K9, yo, ssk, (k2tog, yo, k18, yo, ssk) nine times, k2tog, yo, k9.

Row 22: Purl.

amaryllis entrelac shawl chart 2: (see page 60)

Row 1 (RS): Knit—22 sts.

Row 2 AND ALL WS ROWS: Purl to last st, p2tog joining to next st of prev section.

Rows 3, 5, & 7: Knit.

Row 9: K6, k3tog, yo, k1, yo, 2-2, yo, k1, yo, sk2p, k6.

Row 11: K5, k3tog, yo, k1, yo, (2-2) twice, yo, k1, yo, sk2p, k5.

Row 13: K4, k3tog, yo, k1, yo, (2-2) three times, yo, k1, yo, sk2p, k4.

Row 15: K3, k3tog, yo, k1, yo, (2-2) four times, yo, k1, yo, sk2p, k3.

Row 17: K2, k3tog, yo, k1, yo, (2-2) five times, yo, k1, yo, sk2p, k2.

Row 19: K1, k3tog, yo, k1, yo, (2-2) six times, yo, k1, yo, sk2p, k1.

Row 21: K3, yo, sk2p, yo, (2-2) twice, k2, (2-2) twice, yo, k3tog, yo, k3.

Row 23: K4, yo, sk2p, yo, 2-2, k4, 2-2, yo, k3tog, yo, k4.

Row 25: K10, nupp twice, k10.

Row 27: K9, nupp, 2-2, nupp, k9.

Row 29: K10, nupp twice, k10.

Row 31, 33, & 35: Knit.

Row 37: K5, nupp twice, k8, nupp twice, k5.

Row 39: K4, nupp, 2-2, nupp, k6, nupp, 2-2, nupp, k4.

Row 41: K5, nupp twice, k8, nupp twice, k5.

Row 43: Knit.

Row 44: As Row 2.

amaryllis entrelac shawl chart 3: (see page 60)

Note
At the end of every RS row, you will use ssk to join this diamond to the rem sts of previous tier or lace edge.

Row 1 (RS): K21, ssk—22 sts.

Row 2 and all WS rows: Purl.

Row 3: K21, ssk.

Row 5: K21, ssk.

Row 7: K6, k2tog, yo, k1, yo, k2tog, k1, ssk, yo, k1, ssk twice, k4, ssk.

Row 9: K5, k2tog, yo, k1, yo, nupp, k2tog, k1, ssk, nupp, yo, k1, yo, ssk, k3, ssk.

Row 11: K4, k2tog, yo, k1, yo, nupp, k1, k2tog, k1, ssk, k1, nupp, yo, k1, yo, ssk, k2, ssk.

Row 13: K3, k2tog, yo, k1, yo, nupp, twice, k1, k2tog, k1, ssk, k2, nupp, yo, k1, yo, ssk, k1, ssk.

Row 15: K2, k2tog, yo, k1, yo, nupp, k3, k2tog, k1, ssk, k3, nupp, yo, k1, yo, ssk twice.

Row 17: K4, nupp, k13, nupp, k2, ssk.

Row 19: K9, k2tog, yo, k1, yo, ssk, k7, ssk.

Row 21: K8, k2tog, (k1, yo) twice, k1, ssk, k6, ssk.

Row 23: K7, k2tog, k2, yo, k1, yo, k2, ssk, k5, ssk.

Row 25: K6, k2tog, k3, yo, k1, yo, k3, ssk, k4, ssk.

Row 27: K5, k2tog, k4, yo, k1, yo, k4, ssk, k3, ssk.

Row 29: K4, k2tog, k5, yo, k1, yo, k5, ssk, k2, ssk.

Row 31: K5, k2tog, yo, ssk, k2, yo, k1, yo, k3, yo, ssk, k3, ssk.

Row 33: K4, k2tog, yo, k1, yo, ssk, k2tog, yo, k1, yo, k2, yo, k1, yo, ssk, k2, ssk.

Row 35: K3, k2tog, yo, k3, yo, ssk, k4, yo, k3, yo, ssk, k1, ssk.

Row 37: K2, k2tog, yo, k5, yo, ssk, k2, yo, k5, yo, ssk twice.

Row 39: K10, yo, sk2p, yo, k8, ssk.

Row 41: K21, ssk.

Row 43: K21, ssk.

Row 44: Purl.

amaryllis entrelac shawl edging chart (see page 61)

Row 1 (RS): K1, yo, (k19, ssk, k2tog, k19, yo, k2, yo) nine times, k19, ssk, k2tog, k19, yo, k1.

Row 2 AND ALL WS ROWS: Purl.

Row 3: K2, (yo, k18, ssk, k2tog, k18,

yo, k4) nine times, yo, k18, ssk, k2tog, k18, yo, k2.

Row 5: K1, yo, (ssk, yo, k17, ssk, k2tog, k17, yo, k2tog, yo, k2, yo) nine times, ssk, yo, k17, ssk, k2tog, k17, yo, k2tog, yo, k1.

Row 7: K2, (yo, ssk, yo, k16, ssk, k2tog, k16, yo, k2tog, yo, k4) nine times, yo, ssk, yo, k16, ssk, k2tog, k16, yo, k2tog, yo, k2.

Row 9: K2, (k1, yo, ssk, yo, k15, ssk, k2tog, k15, yo, k2tog, yo, k5) nine times, k1, yo, ssk, yo, k15, ssk, k2tog, k15, yo, k2tog, yo, k3.

Row 11: K2, (k2, yo, ssk, yo, k14, ssk, k2tog, k14, yo, k2tog, yo, k6) nine times, k2, yo, ssk, yo, k14, ssk, k2tog, k14, yo, k2tog, yo, k4.

Row 13: K2, (k3, yo, ssk, yo, k13, ssk, k2tog, k13, yo, k2tog, yo, k7) nine times, k3, yo, ssk, yo, k13, ssk, k2tog, k13, yo, k2tog, yo, k5.

Row 15: K2, (k4, yo, ssk, yo, k12, ssk, k2tog, k12, yo, k2tog, yo, k8) nine times, k4, yo, ssk, yo, k12, ssk, k2tog, k12, yo, k2tog, yo, k6.

Row 17: K2, (k5, yo, ssk, yo, k11, ssk, k2tog, k11, yo, k2tog, yo, k9) nine times, k5, yo, ssk, yo, k11, ssk, k2tog, k11, yo, k2tog, yo, k7.

Row 19: K2, (k6, yo, ssk, yo, k10, ssk, k2tog, k10, yo, k2tog, yo, k7, nupp twice, k1) nine times, k6, yo, ssk, yo, k10, ssk, k2tog, k10, yo, k2tog, yo, k8.

Row 21: K2, (k7, yo, ssk, yo, k9, ssk, k2tog, k9, yo, k2tog, yo, k7, nupp, 2-2, nupp) nine times, k7, yo, ssk, yo, k9, ssk, k2tog, k9, yo, k2tog, yo, k9.

Row 23: K2, (k8, yo, ssk, yo, k8, ssk, k2tog, k8, yo, k2tog, yo, k9, nupp twice, k1) nine times, k8, yo, ssk, yo, k8, ssk, k2tog, k8, yo, k2tog, yo, k10.

Row 25: K2, (k9, yo, ssk, yo, k7, ssk, k2tog, k7, yo, k2tog, yo, k13) nine times, k9, yo, ssk, yo, k7, ssk, k2tog, k7, yo, k2tog, yo, k11.

Row 27: K2, (k1, nupp twice, k7, yo, ssk, yo, k6, ssk, k2tog, k6, yo, k2tog, yo, k7, nupp twice, k5) nine times, k1, nupp twice, k7, yo, ssk, yo, k6, ssk, k2tog, k6, yo, k2tog, yo, k7, nupp twice, k3.

Row 29: K2, (nupp, 2-2, nupp, k7, yo, ssk, yo, k5, ssk, k2tog, k5, yo, k2tog, yo, k7, nupp, 2-2, nupp, k4) nine times, nupp, 2-2, nupp, k7, yo, ssk, yo, k5, ssk, k2tog, k5, yo, k2tog, yo, k7, nupp, 2-2, nupp, k2.

Row 31: K2, (k1, nupp twice, k9, yo, ssk, yo, k4, ssk, k2tog, k4, yo, k2tog, yo, k9, nupp twice, k5) nine times, k1, nupp twice, k9, yo, ssk, yo, k4, ssk, k2tog, k4, yo, k2tog, yo, k9, nupp twice, k3.

Row 33: K2, (k13, yo, ssk, yo, k3, ssk, k2tog, k3, yo, k2tog, yo, k17) nine times, k13, yo, ssk, yo, k3, ssk, k2tog, k3, yo, k2tog, yo, k15.

Row 35: K2, (k14, yo, ssk, yo, k2, ssk, k2tog, k2, yo, k2tog, yo, k15, nupp twice, k1) 9 times, k14, yo, ssk, yo, k2, ssk, k2tog, k2, yo, k2tog, yo, k16.

Row 37: K2, (k15, yo, ssk, yo, k1, ssk, k2tog, k1, yo, k2tog, yo, k15, nupp, 2-2, nupp) 9 times, k15, yo, ssk, yo, k1, ssk, k2tog, k1, yo, k2tog, yo, k17.

Row 39: K2, (k16, (yo, ssk) twice, (k2tog, yo) twice, k17, nupp twice, k1) 9 times, k16, (yo, ssk) twice, (k2tog, yo) twice, k18.

Row 41: K2, (k17, yo, k1, ssk, k2tog, k1, yo, k21) 9 times, k17, yo, k1, ssk, k2tog, k1, yo, k19.

Row 43: K2, (k18, yo, ssk, k2tog, yo, k22) 9 times, k18, yo, ssk, k2tog, yo, k20.

Notes

Shawl is worked from the bottom up, beginning with the bottom lace edge; shawl body is then attached while you are working entrelac diamonds. Top edging is then picked up and knit across top edge of shawl.

Throughout pattern, slip the first stitch of every row pwise.

WS rows are not charted; all WS rows in chart are purled.

INSTRUCTIONS

bottom lace edge

Note

Bottom lace edge is cast on and knit in one piece; you then begin the first entrelac diamond at the midway point of edging to create point.

CO 440 sts.

Work rows 1–22 of Chart 1, repeating highlighted portion of Chart 1 nine times across.

Break yarn. With RS facing, slip first 220 sts pwise.

shawl body

Tier 1

With RS facing and beg with next st on left needle (221st edging st), join yarn and knit next 22 sts.

Turn work and purl these 22 sts.

*Working on just these 22 sts, work rows 1–44 of Chart 2. Note: WS rows are not charted; all WS rows in Chart 2 are worked (p21, p last st tog with lace edge st, joining diamond).

After completing row 44, do not turn work.

Tier 2 and all even-numbered tiers
Purl next 22 sts from lace edge; turn work.

*Work rows 1–43 of Chart 3 over these 22 sts. *Note:* At the end of every RS row, you will use ssk to join this diamond to the rem sts of previous tier or lace edge (ssk is shown on chart).

After completing Row 43, do not turn work. Pick up and knit 22 sts from remaining edge of Tier 1 diamond. Turn and purl 22.

Rep from * until all diamonds from previous tier have been joined and one diamond has been joined to lace edge. *Note:* Tier 2 has two diamonds, tier 4 has four diamonds, and so on.

Tier 3 and rem odd-numbered tiers
*Work rows 1–44 of Chart 2, joining diamonds to previous tier or lace edge at the end of every WS row as in Tier 1. After competing Row 44, do not turn work; pick up and purl 22 sts from edge of facing diamond from previous tier. Rep from * until all diamonds from previous tier have been joined and one diamond has been joined to lace edge. *Note:* Tier 3 has three diamonds, tier 5 has five diamonds, and so on.

Work Tiers 4 through 9 as above.

edging

With RS facing, k44, *pick up and k 22 sts from Tier 9, k22, rep from * around—440 sts.

Work edging chart over all sts, then BO loosely pwise on Row 44.

FINISHING
Weave in all ends and block piece to measurements.

Amaryllis Entrelac Shawl Chart 1

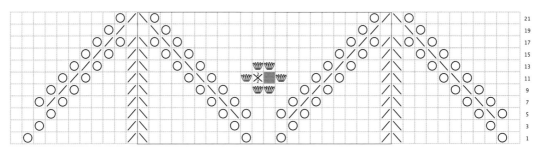

Only odd-numbered rows are charted;
all even-numbered rows are purl across.
Join as noted in pattern.

Amaryllis Entrelac Shawl Chart 2

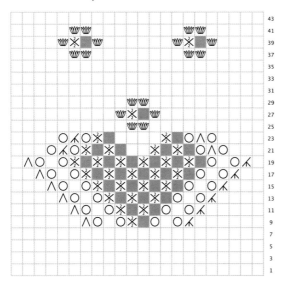

Amaryllis Entrelac Shawl Chart 3

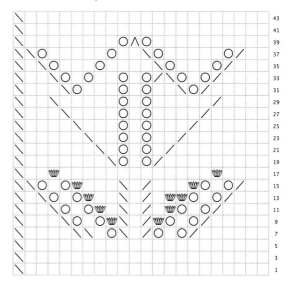

Only odd-numbered rows are charted;
all even-numbered rows are purl across.
Join as noted in pattern.

Amaryllis Entrelac Shawl Edging Chart

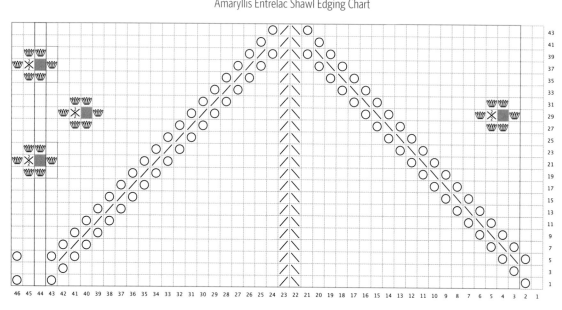

Only odd-numbered rows are charted;
all even-numbered rows are purl across.

☐	RS: knit WS: purl
◯	yo
╱	RS: k2tog WS: p2tog
╲	RS: ssk WS: p2tog tbl
〰	nupp
✕	2 into 2 gathered
■	gray no stitch
☐	repeat
⋏	RS: k3tog WS: p3tog
⋀	RS: sl1, k2tog, psso WS: sl1 wyif, p2tog tbl, psso

montauk sweater

SOMETIMES A TOUCH OF LACE goes a long way. Montauk is a standard top-down raglan pullover, but I've added a lace panel to the raglan lines to add a touch of femininity. The lace panels proceed down the lower body of the sweater, with hourglass shaping to flatter the body. The lace is mirrored in the cuffs and turtleneck. (If you prefer a crew neck, skip the lace edging and cast on the 56 body stitches.) Knit in a bulky wool, Montauk is the sweater you'll reach for on those brisk fall mornings, perfect for a walk in the woods.

SKILL LEVEL

INTERMEDIATE

FINISHED MEASUREMENTS

Bust 40 (46, 52)"/102 (117, 132)cm
To fit bust measurements 36-38 (40-44, 46-50)"

MATERIALS AND TOOLS

Cascade Yarns Eco+ (100% wool; 8.75oz/250g = 478yd/437m): 2 (3, 3) skeins, color mystic purple #2450—approx 800 (1000, 1200) yd/732 (914, 1097)m of bulky weight yarn **(5)**

Knitting needles: 6mm (size 10 U.S.) 16" and 24" circular needles or size to obtain gauge

Stitch markers

Waste yarn (for provisional cast on)

Spare dpn

Tapestry needle

GAUGE

14 sts/21 rows = 4"/10cm over St st after blocking
Always take time to check your gauge.

Special Abbreviations
dec4to1: k2tog, k2tog, pass the 1st rem st over 2nd rem st—3 sts decr'd

PATTERN STITCHES

montauk sweater chart 1 (worked in the rnd): (see page 67)

NOTE: St count changes over Chart 1.

RND 1 (RS): Ssk, yo, k5, (yo, k1) three times—13 sts.

RND 2 and all even-numbered rnds: K.

RND 3: Ssk, yo, ssk, k1, (k2tog, yo) twice, k3, yo, k1.

RND 5: Ssk, yo, sk2p, yo, k2tog, yo, k5, yo, k1.

RND 7: Sk2p, yo, k2tog, yo, k1, yo, ssk, k1, k2tog, yo, ssk—11 sts.

RND 9: K1, k2tog, yo, k3, yo, sk2p, yo, ssk—10 sts.

RND 10: K.

montauk sweater chart 2 (worked in the rnd): (see page 67)

Note: St count changes over Chart 2.

Rnd 1 (RS): (K1, yo) three times, k5, yo, k2tog—13 sts.

Rnd 2 and all even-numbered rnds: K.

Rnd 3: K1, yo, k3, (yo, ssk) twice, k2, yo, k2tog.

Rnd 5: K1, yo, k5, yo, ssk, yo, sk2p, yo, k2tog.

Rnd 7: K2tog, yo, ssk, k1, k2tog, yo, k1, yo, ssk, yo, sk2p—11 sts.

Rnd 9: K2tog, yo, sk2p, yo, k3, yo, ssk, k1—10 sts.

Rnd 10: K.

montauk sweater chart 3 (worked in the rnd): (see page 67)

Note: St count changes over Chart 3.

Rnd 1 (RS): Ssk, yo, k5, (yo, k1) twice, yo, ssk, k2, k2tog, (yo, k1) twice, yo, k5, yo, k2tog—28 sts.

Rnd 2 & all even-numbered rnds: K.

Rnd 3: Ssk, yo, ssk, k1, (k2tog, yo) twice, k3, yo, k4, yo, k3, (yo, ssk) twice, k1, k2tog, yo, k2tog.

Rnd 5: Ssk, yo, sk2p, yo, k2tog, yo, k5, yo, k4, yo, k5, yo, ssk, yo, sk2p, yo, k2tog.

Rnd 7: Sk2p, yo, k2tog, yo, k1, yo, ssk, k1, k2tog, yo, ssk, k2, k2tog, yo, ssk, k1, k2tog, yo, k1, yo, ssk, yo, sk2p—24 sts.

Rnd 9: K1, k2tog, yo, k3, yo, sk2p, yo, sk2p twice, yo, sk2p, yo, k3, yo, ssk, k1—20 sts.

Rnd 11: Ssk, yo, k5, (yo, k1) twice, yo, k2, (yo, k1) twice, yo, k5, yo, k2tog—26 sts.

Rnd 13: Ssk, yo, ssk, k1, (k2tog, yo) twice, k3, yo, k2, yo, k3, (yo, ssk) twice, k2, yo, k2tog.

Rnd 15: Ssk, yo, sk2p, yo, k2tog, yo, k5, yo, k2, yo, k5, yo, ssk, yo, sk2p, yo, k2tog.

Rnd 17: Sk2p, yo, k2tog, yo, k1, yo, ssk, k1, (k2tog, yo, ssk) twice, k1, k2tog, yo, k1, yo, ssk, yo, sk2p—22 sts.

Rnd 19: K1, k2tog, yo, k4, sk2p, yo, dec4to1, yo, sk2p, yo, k3, yo, ssk, k1—19 sts.

Rnd 20: K.

montauk sweater chart 4 (worked in the rnd): (see page 67)

Note: St count changes over Chart 4.

Rnd 1 (RS): Ssk, yo, k5, (yo, k1) five times, yo, k5, yo, k2tog—25 sts.

Rnd 2 & all even-numbered rnds: K.

Rnd 3: Ssk, yo, ssk, k1, (k2tog, yo) twice, k3, yo, k1, yo, k3, (yo, ssk) twice, k1, k2tog, yo, k2tog.

Rnd 5: Ssk, yo, sk2p, yo, k2tog, yo, k5, yo, k1, yo, k5, yo, ssk, yo, sk2p, yo, k2tog.

Rnd 7: Sk2p, yo, k2tog, yo, k1, yo, ssk, k1, k2tog, yo, sk2p, yo, ssk, k1, k2tog, yo, k1, yo, ssk, yo, sk2p—21 sts.

Rnd 9: K1, k2tog, yo, k3, (yo, sk2p) three times, yo, k3, yo, ssk, k1—19 sts.

Rnd 10: K.

montauk sweater chart/cuff chart (worked flat): (see page 67)

Note: St count changes over chart.

Row 1 (RS): K1, ssk, yo, k5, (yo, k1) twice, yo, k2—15 sts.

Row 2 & all WS rows: P.

Row 3: K1, ssk, yo, ssk, k1, (k2tog, yo) twice, k3, yo, k2.

Row 5: K1, ssk, yo, sk2p, yo, k2tog, yo, k5, yo, k2.

Row 7: K1, sk2p, yo, k2tog, yo, k1, yo, ssk, k1, k2tog, yo, ssk, k1—13 sts.

Row 9: K2, k2tog, yo, k3, yo, sk2p, yo, ssk, k1—12 sts.

Row 10: P.

Note
Montauk is constructed from the top down, beginning with the collar. The collar is knit side to side and then grafted into a tube; the body is picked up around the bottom edge of collar and knit in the round.

INSTRUCTIONS

collar

With waste yarn and provisional cast-on method, CO 12 sts.

Join working yarn and purl 1 row.

Beg with a RS row, work Collar/Cuff Chart a total of 7 times.

Remove waste yarn at cast-on edge and place sts on spare dpn; graft center back seam.

body

Pick up and knit 56 sts across long edge of collar. Join for working in the round, being careful not to twist. Place marker to show beg of rnd.

Set-up row: K6 (for front), place marker, k10 (Chart 1), PM, k2 (sleeve), PM, p10 (Chart 2), PM, K6 (for back), place marker, k10 (Chart 1), PM, k2 (sleeve), PM, p10 (Chart 2).

Note

You will maintain first 10-st section in Chart 1 pattern, second 10-st section in Chart 2 pattern, third in Chart 1 pattern, and fourth in Chart 2 pattern; do not increase in these sections.

Begin raglan shaping

RND 1: *YO, k to marker, yo, sm, work Row 1 of Chart 1, sm, yo, k to marker, yo, sm, work Row 1 of Chart 2, sm, rep from * once more—64 sts.

RND 2: K.

REP RNDS 1 & 2 19 (24, 29) more times, working successive rows of Charts 1 and 2 as indicated—216 (256, 296) sts; 46 (56, 66) sts for each of front and back; 42 (52, 62) sts for each sleeve.

Divide for lower body

NEXT RND: *K46 (56, 66), sm, work row 1 of Chart 1, slip next 42 (52, 62) sts to holder for sleeve, PM, CO 4 sts for underarm, PM, work row 1 of Chart 2, rep from * once more—140 (160, 180) sts rem on needle for body.

RND 2: K.

RND 3: *K46 (56, 66), sm, work row 2 of Chart 1, sm, k4, sm, work row 2 of Chart 2, sm, rep from * once more.

REP RNDS 2 & 3 three more times, then knit one round.

Begin waist shaping

Note

For this section, you will work front sts to marker, slip marker, then work Chart 3 over the next 24 sts (formerly the 10 Chart 1 sts, 4 underarm sts, and 10 Chart 2 sts), then work sleeve and second half of body sts in the same manner). Remove second, third, sixth, and seventh markers on first round.

NEXT RND: *K to m, sm, work Row 1 of Chart 3 over next 24 sts removing markers that set off 4 underarm sts on first rnd, rep from * to end.

RND 2: K.

Cont in this manner, working each successive row of Chart 3 until you have worked one full repeat of Chart 3—130 (150, 170) sts. Note that even-numbered rows are not charted and are knit.

NEXT RND: *K to m, sm, work Row 1 of Chart 4 over next 24 sts, sm, rep from * to end of rnd.

Row 2: K.

Cont in this manner, working each successive row of Chart 4 until you have worked a total of five full repeats of Chart 4 or until piece is desired length ending with Row 10 of Chart 4. Note that even-numbered rows are not charted and are knit.

BO all sts loosely knitwise.

sleeve (make 2)

CO 3 sts, with RS facing knit across 42 (52, 62) sleeves sts from holder, CO 3 sts—48 (58, 68) sts.

Place marker and join to work in the rnd.

RNDS 1–5: K.

RND 6: K1, ssk, k to last 3 sts, k2tog—46 (56. 66) sts.

Rep these 6 rnds until 26 (34, 36) sts rem.

K 3 rnds, decr 6 (4, 6) sts evenly on last rnd—20 (30, 30) sts.

cuff

Note

Cuff is worked flat and perpendicular to sleeve sts, joining to live sleeve sts at end of every WS rnd, then seaming it.

CO 12 sts. Turn.

NEXT ROW (WS): P11, p last cuff st tog with first sleeve st, turn.

NEXT ROW (RS): Work row 1 of Collar/Cuff Chart over 12 cuff sts only, then turn.

Row 2: P11, p last cuff st tog with next sleeve st, turn.

Cont in this manner, working each successive row of Collar/Cuff Chart until you have worked 4 (6, 6) full repeats.

BO 12 sts. Seam bound-off edge of cuff to cast-on edge of cuff.

FINISHING

Weave in all ends and block piece as desired.

Montauk Sweater Chart 1

Montauk Sweater Chart 2

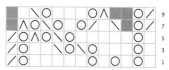

Montauk Sweater Chart 3

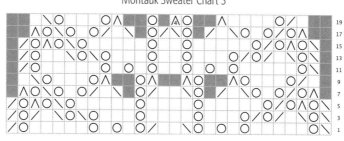

Montauk Sweater Chart 4

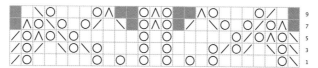

Montauk Sweater Collar/Cuff Chart

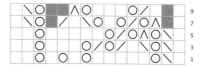

	RS: knit WS: purl
$\bigcirc$	yo
$/$	RS: k2tog WS: p2tog
$\wedge$	RS: sl1, k2tog, psso WS: sl1 wyif, p2tog tbl, psso
$\backslash$	RS: ssk WS: p2tog tbl
▮	gray no stitch
/4\	decrease 4 to 1

Only odd-numbered rows are charted;
all even-numbered rows are knit across.

peony tam

KNITTED COUNTERPANES—SQUARES OR STRIPS OF KNITTING that usually are stitched together as a knitted quilt or bedspread—were popular in the early nineteenth century. For Peony, I started with a traditional counterpane motif and added a fifth section to create a circle rather than a square. Knitting a hat from the center out can be fiddly, and so I recommend the Belly Button cast on (explained below) as a way to simplify the process. Blocking the tam over an 8" dinner plate ensures a perfectly circular tam.

SKILL LEVEL

INTERMEDIATE

FINISHED MEASUREMENTS

Circumference at brim: approx 7"/18cm unstretched (ribbed brim stretches to fit most adult heads)
Diameter of crown: approx 8"/20cm after blocking

MATERIALS AND TOOLS

SMC Extra Merino (100% merino; 1.75oz/50g = 140yd/130m): 2 skeins, color jeansblau #54— approx 218yd/200m of dk weight yarn (3)

Knitting needles: 3.75mm (size 5 U.S.) 24" circular needle and dpns or size to get gauge

3mm (size 3 U.S.) 16" circular needle or two sizes smaller than above

Waste yarn in contrasting color for provisional cast on

Stitch markers

GAUGE

Using larger needles and Chart 2, 19 sts/16 rnds = 4"/10cm after blocking
Always take time to check your gauge.

Special Abbreviations

I-cord: Knit 10 sts, slide sts to other end of dpn, but do not turn work; rep until cord is desired length.

Notes

Tam is knit from the center of the crown outward, ending with the brim. Begin by knitting an I-cord, using dpns and waste yarn; then switch to working yarn as instructed. Switch to circular needle when circumference of work is big enough and place new marker in a different color to show beg of rnd. Markers are used to divide stitch repeats in lace pattern (there are a total of five stitch repeats in each round); slip them as you come to them.

INSTRUCTIONS

Using waste yarn and dpns, CO 10 sts. Work I-cord in waste yarn for 1 1/2"/4cm, then break off waste yarn. Join working yarn, leaving 10"/25cm tail, and knit across 10 sts.

Now arrange 10 sts on dpns as follows:

NEEDLE 1: K2, place marker, k2;

NEEDLE 2: K2, PM, k2;

NEEDLE 3: K2.

Begin lace pattern

Note

Lace patt is also charted (see page 71); repeat each row of Chart 1 five times for each round.

R<small>ND</small> 1: *K1, yo, rep from * to end—20 sts.

R<small>ND</small> 2 and all even-numbered rnds: Knit.

R<small>ND</small> 3: *(K1, yo) twice, ssk, yo, rep from * to end—30 sts.

R<small>ND</small> 5: *K1, yo, k2tog, yo, k1, yo, ssk, yo, rep from * to end—40 sts.

R<small>ND</small> 7: *K1, yo, k2, yo, sk2p, yo, k2, yo, rep from * to end—50 sts.

R<small>ND</small> 9: *K1, yo, k1, k2tog, yo, k3, yo, ssk, k1, yo, rep from * to end—60 sts.

R<small>ND</small> 11: *K1, yo, k3, yo, k1, sk2p, k1, yo, k3, yo, rep from * to end—70 sts.

R<small>ND</small> 13: *K1, yo, k2, k2tog, yo, k5, yo, ssk, k2, yo, rep from * to end—80 sts.

R<small>ND</small> 15: *K1, yo, k4, yo, k2, sk2p, k2, yo, k4, yo, rep from * to end—90 sts.

R<small>ND</small> 17: *K1, yo, k3, k2tog, yo, k7, yo, ssk, k3, yo, rep from * to end—100 sts.

R<small>ND</small> 19: *K1, yo, k5, yo, k3, sk2p, k3, yo, k5, yo, rep from * to end—110 sts.

R<small>ND</small> 21: *K1, yo, k4, k2tog, yo, k9, yo, ssk, k4, yo, rep from * to end—120 sts.

R<small>ND</small> 23: *K1, yo, k6, yo, k4, sk2p, k4, yo, k6, yo, rep from * to end—130 sts.

R<small>ND</small> 25: *K1, yo, k5, k2tog, yo, k11, yo, ssk, k5, yo, rep from * to end—140 sts.

R<small>ND</small> 27: *K1, yo, k7, yo, k5, sk2p, k5, yo, k7, yo, rep from * to end—150 sts.

R<small>ND</small> 29: *K1, yo, k6, k2tog, yo, k1, yo, ssk, k7, k2tog, yo, k1, yo, ssk, k6, yo, rep from * to end—160 sts.

R<small>ND</small> 31: *K1, yo, k6, k2tog, yo, k3, yo, ssk, k5, k2tog, yo, k3, yo, ssk, k6, yo, rep from * to end—170 sts.

R<small>ND</small> 33: *K1, (yo, k1, yo, ssk, k3, k2tog, yo, k1, yo, sk2p) twice, yo, k1, yo, ssk, k3, k2tog, yo, k1, yo, rep from * to end—180 sts.

R<small>ND</small> 35: *Ssk, k2, yo, ssk, k1, k2tog, yo, k3, yo, rep from * to end—180 sts.

R<small>ND</small> 36: Knit, removing all markers except marker that shows beg of rnd.

Begin edging pattern

Note

Edging patt appears in Chart 2; repeat each row of Chart 2 45 times for each round.

R<small>ND</small> 37: *Sk2p, yo, k1, yo, rep from * to end—180 sts.

R<small>ND</small> 36: Knit.

R<small>ND</small> 39: *Ssk, k2, yo, rep from * to end—180 sts.

R<small>ND</small> 40: Knit.

R<small>NDS</small> 41–48: Rep rounds 37–40 twice more.

Switch to smaller needles.

R<small>ND</small> 49: *Sk2p, k1, rep from * to end—90 sts.

R<small>ND</small> 50: *K2, p1, rep from * to end.

Repeat Rnd 50 six more times, then BO loosely in rib patt.

FINISHING

Carefully remove waste yarn from provisional cast on, threading tail from working yarn through each live st as you go. Pull to close opening and weave in all ends. Block.

Peony Tam Chart 1

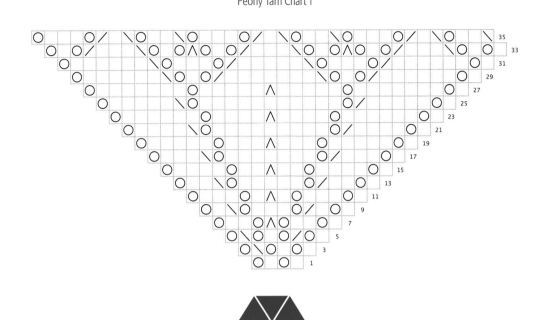

Peony Tam Chart 2

⬜ knit

Ⓞ yo

🔲 gray no stitch

╲ RS: ssk
　 WS: p2tog tbl

╱ RS: k2tog
　 WS: p2tog

⋀ RS: sl1, k2tog, psso
　 WS: sl1 wyif, p2tog tbl, psso

Only odd-numbered rows are charted;
all even-numbered rows are knit across.

squares

THE SQUARE CAN BE SHAPED in a variety of ways, as I explore in this chapter. Wanderlust is constructed from triangles, while Keira is knit from side-to side. Holly explores a traditional quilting shape to create a square shawl. Lea is also a square, which through the magic of drape and blocking becomes a form-fitting top.

holly shawl

IF YOU'RE A QUILTER, you're familiar with traditional log cabin quilts, easily the most recognizable and traditional quilt pattern. Log cabin patterns begin with a center shape, usually a square, and are built by sewing strips around that shape. Holly is a knitted log cabin "quilt." The central square is a traditional Estonian lace motif that is full of texture and nupps. From there, strips alternate in lace motifs and a cluster stitch motif. Holly is a fun pattern to knit, with the added advantage that you can watch it develop as you bind off each panel.

SKILL LEVEL

INTERMEDIATE

FINISHED MEASUREMENTS

40"/102cm square after blocking

MATERIALS AND TOOLS

Schoppel Wolle Leinen Los (70% wool, 30% linen; 3.5oz/100g = 328yd/300m): 3 skeins, color #980—approx 900yd/823m of DK weight yarn ❸

Knitting needles: 3.75mm (size 5 U.S.) 24" and 47" circular needles or size to obtain gauge

Stitch markers

Tapestry needle

GAUGE

Over Chart 1, 41 sts/66 rows = 9"/23cm square after blocking
Always take time to check your gauge.

Special Abbreviations
2/2: into next 2 sts, work (k2tog, k2tog tbl)
Nupp: see page 13

PATTERN STITCHES

Estonian star stitch (odd number of sts):

Row 1 (RS): K1, *2/2, rep from * to last 2 sts, k2.

Row 2 (WS): Purl.

Row 3: K2, *2/2, rep from * to last st, k1.

Row 4: Purl.

holly shawl chart 1 (center square): (see page 82)

Row 1 (RS): Knit.

Row 2 and all WS rows: Purl.

Row 5: K7, k2tog, yo, k3, yo, ssk, k13, k2tog, yo, k3, yo, ssk, k7.

Row 7: K9, yo, sk2p, yo, k17, yo, sk2p, yo, k9.

Row 9: K9, k2tog, yo, k19, yo, ssk, k9.

Row 11: K8, k2tog, yo, k10, nupp, k10, yo, ssk, k8.

Row 13: K7, k2tog, yo, k10, nupp, k1, nupp, k10, yo, ssk, k7.

Row 15: K6, k2tog, yo, k10, nupp, k3, nupp, k10, yo, ssk, k6.

Row 17: K5, k2tog, yo, k6, nupp twice, (k3, nupp) twice, k3, nupp twice, k6, yo, ssk, k5.

Row 19: K4, k2tog, yo, k6, nupp, k2, nupp, k3, nupp, k1, nupp, k3, nupp, k2, nupp, k6, yo, ssk, k4.

Row 21: K3, k2tog, yo, k6, nupp, k4, (nupp, k3) twice, nupp, k4, nupp, k6, yo, ssk, k3.

Row 23: K2, k2tog, yo, k1, yo, ssk, k5, nupp, k2, nupp, k9, nupp, k2, nupp, k6, yo, k1, yo, ssk, k2.

Row 25: K1, k2tog, yo, k3, yo, ssk, k5, nupp twice, k2, (k2tog, yo) three times, k3, nupp twice, k6, yo, k1, sk2p, k1, yo, k2.

Row 27: K2, yo, k1, sk2p, k1, yo, k9, (k2tog, yo) four times, k10, yo, k1, sk2p, k1, yo, k2.

Row 29: K2, yo, k1, sk2p, k1, yo, k3, nupp twice, k3, (k2tog, yo) five times, k4, nupp twice, k3, yo, k1, sk2p, k1, yo, k2.

Row 31: K2, yo, k1, sk2p, k1, yo, (k2, nupp) twice, k3, (k2tog, yo) four times, k4, (nupp, k2) twice, yo, k1, sk2p, k1, yo, k2.

Row 33: K3, yo, sk2p, yo, k2, nupp, k4, nupp, k1, (k2tog, yo) five times, k2, nupp, k4, nupp, k2, yo, sk2p, yo, k3.

Row 35: K3, yo, sk2p, yo, k3, nupp, k2, nupp, k3, (k2tog, yo) four times, k4, nupp, k2, nupp, k3, yo, sk2p, yo, k3.

Row 37: K2, yo, k1, sk2p, k1, yo, k3, nupp twice, k3, (k2tog, yo) five times, k4, nupp twice, k3, yo, k1, sk2p, k1, yo, k2.

Row 39: K2, yo, k1, sk2p, k1, yo, k9, (k2tog, yo) four times, k10, yo, k1, sk2p, k1, yo, k2.

Row 41: K2, yo, k1, sk2p, k1, yo, k6, nupp twice, k2, (k2tog, yo) three times, k3, nupp twice, k6, yo, k1, sk2p, k1, yo, k2.

Row 43: K3, yo, sk2p, yo, k6, nupp, k2, nupp, k9, nupp, k2, nupp, k7, k2tog, yo, k3.

Row 45: K4, yo, ssk, k5, nupp, k4, (nupp, k3) twice, nupp, k4, nupp, k5, k2tog, yo, k4.

Row 47: K5, yo, ssk, k5, nupp, k2, nupp, k3, nupp, k1, nupp, k3, nupp, k2, nupp, k5, k2tog, yo, k5.

Row 49: K6, yo, ssk, k5, nupp twice, (k3, nupp) twice, k3, nupp twice, k5, k2tog, yo, k6.

Row 51: K7, yo, ssk, k9, nupp, k3, nupp, k9, k2tog, yo, k7.

Row 53: K8, yo, ssk, k9, nupp, k1, nupp, k9, k2tog, yo, k8.

Row 55: K9, yo, ssk, k9, nupp, k9, k2tog, yo, k9.

Row 57: K10, yo, ssk, k17, k2tog, yo, k10.

Row 59: K9, yo, sk2p, yo, k17, yo, sk2p, yo, k9.

Row 61: K7, k2tog, yo, k3, yo, ssk, k13, k2tog, yo, k3, yo, ssk, k7.

Row 63: K9, yo, sk2p, yo, k17, yo, sk2p, yo, k9.

Row 65: Knit.

holly shawl chart 2 (strips 5–8): (see page 82)

Row 1 (RS): K2, yo, ssk, *k1, yo, k2tog, k1, yo, ssk, rep from * to last 3 sts, k3.

Row 2 and all WS rows: Purl.

Row 3: K3, yo, *ssk, k1, k2tog, yo, k1, yo, rep from * to last 4 sts, ssk, k2.

Row 5: K4, *yo, sk2p, yo, k3, rep from * to last 3 sts, yo, ssk, k1.

Row 7: K2, yo, k2tog, *k1, yo, ssk, k1, yo, k2tog, rep from * to last 3 sts, k3.

Row 9: K3, k2tog, *yo, k1, yo, ssk, k1, k2tog, rep from * to last 2 sts, yo, k2.

Row 11: K2, k2tog, yo, *k3, yo, sk2p, yo, rep from * to last 3 sts, k3.

holly shawl chart 3 (strips 13–16): (see page 82)

Row 1 (RS): K2, yo, ssk, k1, *k2, k2tog, yo, k1, yo, ssk, k1, rep from * to last 6 sts, k2, k2tog, yo, k2.

Row 2 & all WS rows: Purl.

Row 3: K3, yo, ssk, *k1, k2tog, yo, k3, yo, ssk, rep from * to last 6 sts, k1, k2tog, yo, k3.

Row 5: K2, k2tog, yo, k1, *k2, yo, ssk, k1, k2tog, yo, k1, rep from * to last 6 sts, k2, yo, ssk, k2.

Row 7: K1, k2tog, yo, k2, *k3, yo, sk2p, yo, k2, rep from * to last 6 sts, k3, yo, ssk, k1.

Row 9: K3, k2tog, yo, *k1, yo, ssk, k3, k2tog, yo, rep from * to last 6 sts, k1, yo, ssk, k3.

Row 11: K2, k2tog, yo, k1, *k2, yo, ssk, k1, k2tog, yo, k1, rep from * to last 6 sts, k2, yo, ssk, k2.

Row 13: K3, yo, ssk, *k1, k2tog, yo, k3, yo, ssk, rep from * to last 6 sts, k1, k2tog, yo, k3.

Row 15: K4, yo, *sk2p, yo, k5, yo, rep from * to last 7 sts, sk2p, yo, k4.

Row 17: K2, yo, ssk, k1, *k2, k2tog, yo, k1, yo, ssk, k1, rep from * to last 6 sts, k2, k2tog, yo, k2.

Row 19: K3, yo, ssk, *k1, k2tog, yo, k3, yo, ssk, rep from * to last 6 sts, k1, k2tog, yo, k3.

Row 21: K2, k2tog, yo, k1, *k2, yo, ssk, k1, k2tog, yo, k1, rep from * to last 6 sts, k2, yo, ssk, k2.

Row 23: K1, k2tog, yo, k2, *k3, yo, sk2p, yo, k2, rep from * to last 6 st, k3, yo, ssk, k1.

Row 24: Purl.

holly shawl edging chart: (see page 83)

Rnd 1: *K1, (yo, k2tog) four times, yo, k1, [(yo, ssk) three times, yo, sk2p, (yo, k2tog) three times, yo, k1] repeat between [ ] six times, (yo, ssk) four times, yo, sm, rep from * three more times—464 sts.

Rnd 2 and all even-numbered rnds: Knit.

Rnd 3: *K1, yo, k2, (k2tog, yo) three times, k2, [k1, (yo, ssk) three times, k1, (k2tog, yo) three times, k2] repeat between [ ] six times, k1, (yo, ssk) three times, k2, yo, sm, rep from * three more times—472 sts.

Rnd 5: *K1, yo, k4, (k2tog, yo) three times, k1, [(yo, ssk) three times, k3, (k2tog, yo) three times, k1] repeat between [ ] six times, (yo, ssk) three times, k4, yo, sm, rep from * three more times—480 sts.

Rnd 7: *K1, yo, k3, nupp, k2, (k2tog, yo) twice, k2, [k1, (yo, ssk) twice, k2, nupp, k2, (k2tog, yo) twice, k2] repeat between [ ] six times, k1, (yo, ssk) twice, k2, nupp, k3, yo, sm, rep from * three more times—488 sts.

Rnd 9: *K1, yo, k3, nupp, k1, nupp, k2, (k2tog, yo) twice, k1, [(yo, ssk) twice, k2, nupp, k1, nupp, k2, (k2tog, yo) twice, k1] repeat between [ ] six times, (yo, ssk) twice, k2, nupp, k1, nupp, k3, yo, sm, rep from * three more times—496 sts.

Rnd 11: *K1, yo, k5, nupp, k4, k2tog, yo, k2, (k1, yo, ssk, k4, nupp, k4, k2tog, yo, k2) repeat between [ ] six times, k1, yo, ssk, k4, nupp, k5, yo, sm, rep from * three more times—504 sts.

Rnd 13: *K1, yo, k12, k2tog, yo, k1, (yo, ssk, k11, k2tog, yo, k1) repeat between [ ] six times, yo, ssk, k12, yo, sm, rep from * three more times—512 sts.

Rnd 15: *K1, yo, k6, yo, sk2p, yo, k7, (k6, yo, sk2p, yo, k7) six times, k6, yo, sk2p, yo, k6, yo, sm, rep from * three more times—520 sts.

Rnd 17: *K1, yo, k6, yo, ssk, k1, k2tog, yo, k6, (k5, yo, ssk, k1, k2tog, yo, k6) six times, k5, yo, ssk, k1, k2tog, yo, k6, yo, sm, rep from * three more times—528 sts.

Rnd 19: *K1, yo, k6, yo, k1, ssk, k1, k2tog, k1, yo, k5, (k4, yo, k1, ssk, k1, k2tog, k1, yo, k5) repeat between [ ] six times, k4, yo, k1, ssk, k1, k2tog, k1, yo, k6, yo, sm, rep from * three more times—536 sts.

Rnd 21: *K1, yo, k6, yo, k2, ssk, k1, k2tog, k2, yo, k4, (k3, yo, k2, ssk, k1, k2tog, k2, yo, k4) six times, k3, yo, k2, ssk, k1, k2tog, k2, yo, k6, yo, sm, rep from * three more times—544 sts.

Rnd 23: *K1, yo, k6, yo, k3, ssk, k1, k2tog, k3, yo, k3, (k2, yo, k3, ssk, k1, k2tog, k3, yo, k3) six times, k2, yo, k3, ssk, k1, k2tog, k3, yo, k6, yo, sm, rep from * three more times—552 sts.

Rnd 25: *K1, yo, k2tog, k1, yo, k3, yo, k4, ssk, k1, k2tog, k4, yo, k2, (k1, yo, k4, ssk, k1, k2tog, k4, yo, k2) six times, k1, yo, k4, ssk, k1, k2tog, k4, yo, k3, yo, k1, ssk, yo, sm, rep from * three more times—560 sts.

Rnd 27: *K1, yo, k2tog, k3, yo, k1, yo, k6, sk2p, k6, yo, k1, (yo, k6, sk2p, k6, yo, k1) six times, yo, k6, sk2p, k6, yo, k1, yo, k3, ssk, yo, sm, rep from * three more times—568 sts.

Rnd 29: *K1, yo, k2tog, k4, yo, k1, yo, k6, sk2p, k6, yo, k1, (yo, k6, sk2p, k6, yo, k1) six times, yo, k6, sk2p, k6, yo, k1, yo, k4, ssk, yo, sm, rep from * three more times—576 sts.

Rnd 31: *K1, yo, k2tog, k5, yo, k1, yo, k6, sk2p, k6, yo, k1, (yo, k6, sk2p, k6, yo, k1) six times, yo, k6, sk2p, k6, yo, k1, yo, k5, ssk, yo, sm, rep from * three more times—584 sts.

Rnd 33: *Yo, k1, yo, k2tog, k6, yo, k1, yo, k6, sk2p, k6, yo, k1, (yo, k6, sk2p, k6, yo, k1, yo, k7, ssk, sm, rep from * three more times—592 sts.

Rnd 35: *Yo, k3, yo, k2tog, k5, yo, k3, yo, k5, sk2p, k5, yo, k2, (k1, yo, k5, sk2p, k5, yo, k2) six times, k1, yo, k5, sk2p, k5, yo, k3, yo, k6, ssk, sm, rep from * three more times—600 sts.

Rnd 37: *K1, yo, sk2p, yo, k8, yo, sk2p, yo, k13, yo, sk2p, (yo, k13, yo, sk2p) six times, yo, k13, yo, sk2p, yo, k8, sm, rep from * three more times—608 sts.

Rnd 38: Knit.

Note
Shawl is knit modularly, beginning with a center square. Each subsequent section is picked up along an edge of the square, building outward in tiers. If you are having trouble picking up the specified number of sts on the pick-up row, simply increase or decrease as needed on the following (purl) row. After all tiers are complete, the edging is picked up around all four edges of the shawl and knit in the round.

INSTRUCTIONS

tier 1

Center square
CO 41 sts.

SET-UP ROW (WS): Purl.

Work Chart 1, then BO all sts loosely kwise—do not cut yarn or fasten off last st.

Strip 1
Using working yarn and rem st from center square, turn work 90 degrees to right and pick up and knit 34 sts in left selvedge edge—35 sts.

Turn work and purl 1 row.

Beg with a RS row, work 8 rows of Estonian star st.

BO all sts loosely kwise—do not cut yarn or fasten off last st.

Strip 2
Using working yarn and rem st from previous strip, turn work 90 degrees to right and pick up and knit 46 sts in selvedge edge of previous strip and cast-on edge of center square—47 sts.

Turn work and purl 1 row.

Beg with a RS row, work 8 rows of Estonian star st.

BO all sts loosely kwise—do not cut yarn or fasten off last st.

Strip 3
Using working yarn and rem st from previous strip, turn work 90 degrees to right and pick up and knit 40 sts in selvedge edge of previous strip and cast-on edge of center square—41 sts.

Turn work and purl 1 row.

Beg with a RS row, work 8 rows of Estonian star st.

BO all sts loosely kwise—do not cut yarn or fasten off last st.

Strip 4
Using working yarn and rem st from previous strip, turn work 90 degrees to right and pick up and knit 52 sts in selvedge edge of previous strip and cast-on edge of center square—53 sts.

Turn work and purl 1 row.

Beg with a RS row, work 8 rows of Estonian star st.

BO all sts loosely kwise—do not cut yarn or fasten off last st.

tier 2

Using working yarn and rem st from previous strip, turn work 90 degrees to right and pick up and knit 48 sts in selvedge edge of previous strip and cast-on edge of center square—49 sts.

Turn work and purl 1 row.

Work Chart 2 across all sts, rep highlighted sts as needed.

BO all sts loosely kwise—do not cut yarn or fasten off last st.

Work Strips 6, 7, and 8 in the same manner, picking up the designated number of sts below, working 1 purl row, then completing Chart 2 across all sts and binding off without cutting yarn or fastening off last st. When you have completed Strip 8, begin Tier 3.

STRIP 6: CO 60 sts—61 sts total.

STRIP 7: CO 54 sts—55 sts total.

STRIP 8: CO 66 sts—67 sts total.

tier 3

Strip 9
Using working yarn and rem st from previous strip, turn work 90 degrees to right and pick up and knit 64 sts in selvedge edge of previous strip and cast-on edge of center square—65 sts.

Turn work and purl 1 row.

Work 6 rows of Estonian star st.

BO all sts loosely kwise—do not cut yarn or fasten off last st.

Work Strips 10, 11, and 12 in the same manner, picking up the designated number of sts below, working 1 purl row, then completing 6 rows of Estonian star st across all sts and binding off without cutting yarn or fastening off last st. When you have completed Strip 12, begin Tier 4.

STRIP 10: CO 72 sts—73 sts total.

STRIP 11: CO 66 sts—67 sts total.

STRIP 12: CO 76 sts—77 sts total.

tier 4

Strip 13
Using working yarn and rem st from previous strip, turn work 90 degrees to right and pick up and knit 74 sts in selvedge edge of previous strip and cast-on edge of center square—75 sts.

Turn work and purl 1 row.

Work Chart 3 across all sts, rep highlighted sts as needed.

BO all sts loosely kwise—do not cut yarn or fasten off last st.

Work Strips 14, 15, and 16 in the same manner, picking up the designated number of sts below, working 1 purl row, then completing Chart 3 across all sts and binding off without cutting yarn or fastening off last st. When you have completed Strip 12, begin Tier 5.

STRIP 14: CO 90 sts—91 sts total.

STRIP 15: CO 82 sts—83 sts total.

STRIP 16: CO 98 sts—99 sts total.

tier 5

Strip 17

Using working yarn and rem st from previous strip, turn work 90 degrees to right and pick up and knit 98 sts in selvedge edge of previous strip and cast-on edge of center square—99 sts.

Turn work and purl 1 row.

Work 12 rows of Estonian star st.

BO all sts loosely kwise—do not cut yarn or fasten off last st.

Work Strips 18, 19, and 20 in the same manner, picking up the designated number of sts below, working 1 purl row, then completing 12 rows of Estonian star st and binding off without cutting yarn or fastening off last st.

When you have completed Strip 20, work edging.

STRIP 18: CO 106 sts—107 sts total.

STRIP 19: CO 106 sts—107 sts total.

STRIP 20: CO 114 sts—115 sts total.

EDGING

Using working yarn and st rem from Strip 20, turn work 90 degrees to the right, pick up and knit 113 sts from edge of piece, and place marker to show corner; *turn work again and pick up and knit 114 sts from next edge of piece, placing marker to show corner; rep from * for each of two remaining edges of shawl, placing marker at each corner—456 sts.

Begin working Edging Chart: You will work one repeat of the chart over each 114 sts set off by markers, repeating highlighted portion of chart six times within each 114-st section. Note that only odd-numbered rnds are charted; even-numbered rnds are knit. You will increase 8 sts on each odd-numbered rnd—608 sts after working Rnd 37.

BO all sts loosely kwise after Rnd 37 is complete.

FINISHING

Block piece to measurements, pinning out points on edging if desired. Weave in all ends.

Holly Shawl Chart 1

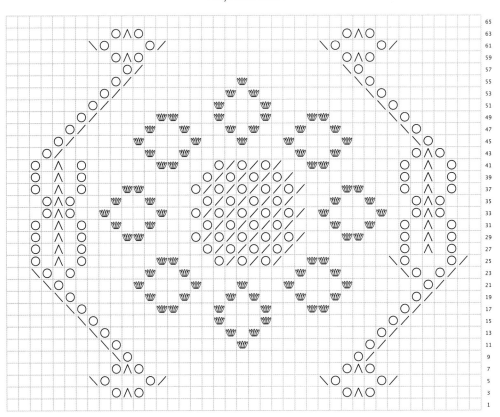

Holly Shawl Chart 2

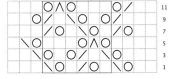

Holly Shawl Chart 3

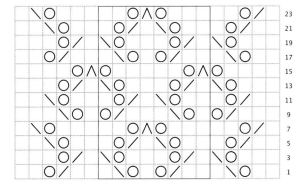

Holly Shawl Edging Chart

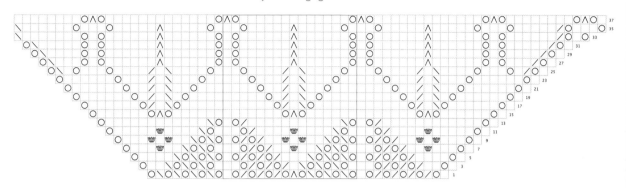

Only odd-numbered rows are charted;
all even-numbered rows are knit around.

☐	RS: knit WS: purl
◯	yo
∧	RS: sl1, k2tog, psso WS: sl1 wyif, p2tog tbl, psso
╱	RS: k2tog WS: p2tog
╲	RS: ssk WS: p2tog tbl
♔	nupp
☐	repeat
▨	gray no stitch

Holly Shawl Schematic

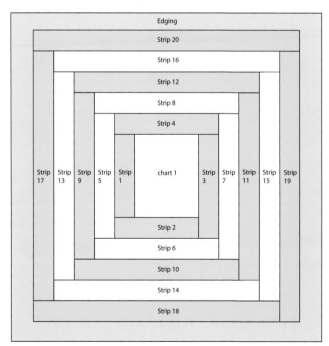

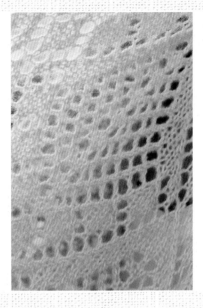

keira wrap

THE LUXURY OF CASHMERE AND SILK and the sturdiness of merino combine to create this soft and dainty piece. Worn as a stole stretched across the shoulders or as a cowl draped around the neck, Keira adds a touch of lightweight warmth. Keira is knit from side to side, with ribbing at either end to gather the lace motif into a graceful shape.

SKILL LEVEL

INTERMEDIATE

FINISHED MEASUREMENTS

36"/91cm long • 12½"/32cm wide

MATERIALS AND TOOLS

Filatura Di Crosa Superior (70% cashmere, 25% silk, 5% extrafine merino; .88oz/25g = 330yd/300m): (A), 1 skein, color petal pink #29— approx 330 yd of lace weight yarn 🔵

Filatura Di Crosa Nirvana (100% extrafine merino superwash; .88 oz/25g = 372yd/340m): (B), 1 skein, color blush #2—approx 330 yd of lace weight yarn 🔵

Knitting needles: 4mm (size 6 U.S.) or size to obtain gauge 3.5mm (size 4 U.S.) or two sizes smaller than above

Eight buttons, ½"/12mm diameter

GAUGE

19 sts/24 rows = 4"/10cm over Chart 1 using larger needles and 1 strand each of A and B held together after blocking
Always take time to check your gauge.

Notes

Garment is worked with 1 strand each of A and B held together throughout.

Only RS rows are charted; all WS rows are purled. Chart begins with Row 7 and ends with Row 58 for continuity with pattern instructions.

Wrap is knit from side to side.

Row 3: K9, yo, sk2p, yo, k17, yo, sk2p, yo, k9.

PATTERN STITCHES

keira lace chart: (see page 87)

Row 7 (RS): K2, *(yo, ssk) four times, k2, k2tog, yo, k3, yo, ssk, k2, (k2tog, yo) four times, k1, rep from * to last st, k1—59 sts.

Row 8 AND ALL WS ROWS: Purl.

Row 9: *K3, (yo, ssk) three times, k2, k2tog, yo, k5, yo, ssk, k2, (k2tog, yo) three times, rep from * to last 3 sts, k3.

Row 11: K2, *(yo, ssk) three times, k2, k2tog, yo, k1, yo, ssk, k1, k2tog, yo, k1, yo, ssk, k2, (k2tog, yo) three times, k1, rep from * to last 2 sts, k2tog, k2.

Row 13: *K3, (yo, ssk) twice, k2, k2tog, yo, k3, yo, sk2p, yo, k3, yo, ssk, k2, (k2tog, yo) twice, rep from * to last 3 sts, k3.

Row 15: K2, *(yo, ssk) twice, k2, k2tog, yo, k11, yo, ssk, k2, (k2tog, yo) twice, k1, rep from * to last st, k1.

Row 17: *K3, yo, ssk, k2, (k2tog, yo, k1, yo, ssk, k1) twice, k2tog, yo, k1, yo, ssk, k2, k2tog, yo, rep from * to last 3 sts, k3.

Row 19: K2, *yo, ssk, k2, k2tog, (yo, k3, yo, sk2p) twice, yo, k3, yo, ssk, k2, k2tog, yo, k1, rep from * to last st, k1.

Row 21: *K5, k2tog, yo, k4, (k2tog, yo) twice, k1, (yo, ssk) twice, k4, yo, ssk, k2, rep from * to last 3 sts, k3.

Row 23: *K4, k2tog, yo, k1, yo, ssk, k1, (k2tog, yo) twice, k3, (yo, ssk) twice, k1, k2tog, yo, k1, yo, ssk, k1, rep from * to last 3 sts, k3.

Row 25: *K3, k2tog, yo, k3, yo, sk2p, (yo, k2tog) twice, yo, k1, (yo, ssk) twice, yo, sk2p, yo, k3, yo, ssk, rep from * to last 3 sts, k3.

Row 27: K1, *k1, k2tog, yo, k4, (k2tog, yo) three times, k3, (yo, ssk) three times, k4, yo, ssk, rep from * to last 2 sts, k2.

Row 29: K1, k2tog, yo, k1, yo, ssk, k1, (k2tog, yo) four times, k1, (yo, ssk) four times, k1, k2tog, yo, k1, yo, sk2p, yo, k1, yo, ssk, k1, (k2tog, yo) four times, k1, (yo, ssk) four times, k1, k2tog, yo, k1, yo, ssk, k1.

Row 31: K1, *k1, yo, ssk, k1, yo, sk2p, (yo, k2tog) three times, yo, k3, (yo, ssk) three times, yo, sk2p, yo, k1, k2tog, yo, rep from * to last 2 sts, k2.

Row 33: *K3, yo, ssk, k2, (k2tog, yo) four times, k1, (yo, ssk) four times, k2, k2tog, yo, rep from * to last 3 sts, k3.

Row 35: *K4, yo, ssk, k2, (k2tog, yo)

three times, k3, (yo, ssk) three times, k2, k2tog, yo, k1, rep from * to last 3 sts, k3.

Row 37: K2, *k2tog, yo, k1, yo, ssk, k2, (k2tog, yo) three times, k1, (yo, ssk) three times, k2, k2tog, yo, k1, yo, ssk, k1, rep from * to last st, k1.

Row 39: K1, k2tog, yo, k3, yo, ssk, k2, (k2tog, yo) twice, k3, (yo, ssk) twice, k2, k2tog, yo, k3, yo, sk2p, yo, k3, yo, ssk, k2, (k2tog, yo) twice, k3, (yo, ssk) twice, k2, k2tog, yo, k3, yo, ssk, k1.

Row 41: *K7, yo, ssk, k2, (k2tog, yo) twice, k1, (yo, ssk) twice, k2, k2tog, yo, k4, rep from * to last 3 sts, k3.

Row 43: K2, *yo, ssk, k1, k2tog, yo, k1, yo, ssk, k2, k2tog, yo, k3, yo, ssk, k2, k2tog, yo, k1, yo, ssk, k1, k2tog, yo, k1, rep from * to last st, k1.

Row 45: *K3, yo, sk2p, yo, k3, yo, ssk, k2, k2tog, yo, k1, yo, ssk, k2, k2tog, yo, k3, yo, sk2p, yo, rep from * to last 3 sts, k3.

Row 47: K1, *k1, (yo, ssk) twice, k4, yo, ssk, k7, k2tog, yo, k4, (k2tog, yo) twice, rep from * to last 2 sts, k2.

Row 49: *K3, (yo, ssk) twice, k1, k2tog, yo, k1, yo, ssk, k5, k2tog, yo, k1, yo, ssk, k1, (k2tog, yo) twice, rep from * to last 3 sts, k3.

Row 51: K1, *k1, (yo, ssk) twice, yo, sk2p, yo, k3, yo, ssk, k3, k2tog, yo, k3, yo, sk2p, (yo, k2tog) twice, yo, rep from * to last 2 sts, k2.

Row 53: *K3, (yo, ssk) three times, k4, yo, ssk, k1, k2tog, yo, k4, (k2tog, yo) three times, rep from * to last 3 sts, k3.

Row 55: K1, *k1, (yo, ssk) four times, k1, k2tog, yo, k1, yo, sk2p, yo, k1, yo, ssk, k1, (k2tog, yo) four times, rep from * to last 2 sts, k2.

Row 57: *K3, (yo, ssk) three times, yo, sk2p, yo, k1, k2tog, yo, k1, yo, ssk, k1, yo, sk2p, (yo, k2tog) three times,

yo, rep from * to last 3 sts, k3.

Row 58: Purl.

INSTRUCTIONS

With smaller needles and one strand of each yarn held tog, CO 35 sts.

Rows 1 & 3 (RS): *K3, p1, rep to last 3 sts, k3.

Rows 2 & 4 (WS): *P3, k1, rep to last 3 sts, p3.

Row 5 (incr row): With larger needles, k3, *(yo, k1) five times, (k1, yo) twice, k2, (yo, k1) five times, k2, rep from * one time—59 sts.

Row 6: Purl.

Begin lace pattern

Rows 7–58: Work one full repeat of Chart 1.

Rows 59–161: Rep chart rows 7–58 twice more.

Rows 163–212: Rep chart rows 7–56 once more.

Row 213 (decr row): *K3, ssk three times, sk2p, k2tog, k3, ssk, sk2p, k2tog three times, rep from * to last 3 sts, k3—35 sts.

Row 214: With smaller needles, *p3, k1, rep from * to last 3 sts, p3.

Row 215 (BUTTONHOLE ROW): K3, *yo, k2tog, k2, rep from * to end.

Row 216: As Row 214.

Row 217: *K3, p1, rep from * to last 3 sts, k3.

BO all sts loosely in rib pattern.

FINISHING

Weave in all ends. Block piece to measurements, taking care not to stretch ribbing.

Sew buttons at cast-on edge opposite buttonholes.

Keira Lace Chart

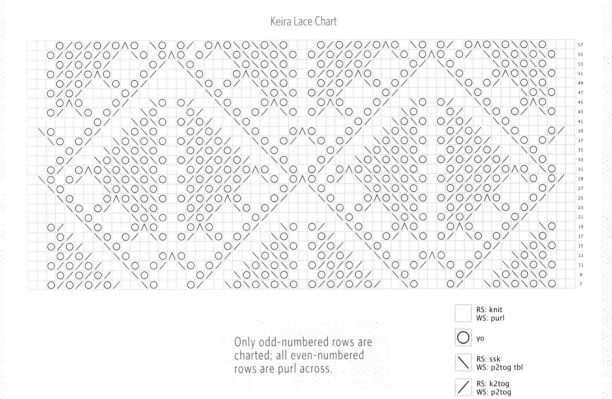

Only odd-numbered rows are charted; all even-numbered rows are purl across.

	RS: knit WS: purl
○	yo
╲	RS: ssk WS: p2tog tbl
╱	RS: k2tog WS: p2tog
⋀	RS: sl1, k2tog, psso WS: sl1 wyif, p2tog tbl, psso

wanderlust shawl

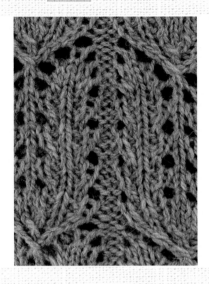

WANDERLUST PROVIDES PROOF that lace shawls don't require tiny yarn and needles. Knit in Aran weight yarn, this is the perfect shawl for a walk in the woods to admire the fall leaves or a winter night by the fire. The classic wool produces great stitch definition and really pops the floral shape that emerges from this stitch motif. This shawl is made of four triangles; think of it as two top-down triangle shawls stuck together. We start with a tab as in a traditional triangle shawl; this allows the shawl to hug the neck as you wear it. Keep in mind that the decreases in Rows 1 and 3 do not have compensating yarn overs, and so the stitch count in each motif changes in those rows.

SKILL LEVEL

EXPERIENCED

FINISHED MEASUREMENTS

Approx. 40"/102cm

MATERIALS AND TOOLS

Cascade Yarns Eco (100% wool; 8.82oz/250g = 478 yd/437m): 2 skeins, color latte #8063—approx 750yd/686m of bulky weight yarn (5)

Knitting needles: 6mm (size 10 U.S.) 47" circular needles or size to obtain gauge

Stitch markers

Tapestry needle

GAUGE

1 repeat of highlighted stitches from Chart 1 (13 sts/22 rows) = 5"/13cm wide × 5"/13cm tall after blocking
Always take time to check your gauge.

PATTERN STITCHES

wanderlust shawl chart 1: (see page 91)

Note

When you are working the first repeat of the lace patt, work bracketed sts one time for each section; when working the second (third, fourth) repeat, work bracketed sts 3 (5, 7) times for each section.

Row 1 (RS): Yo, p2, (yo, ssk, k1, k2tog, k1, ssk, k1, k2tog, yo, p2,) yo.

Row 2 (WS): P1, (k2, p9,) k2, p.

Row 3: Yo, k1, yo, p2, (yo, k1, yo, ssk, sl1, k2tog, psso, k2tog, yo, k1, yo, p2,) yo, k1, yo.

Row 4: P3, (k2, p9,) p1, k1, p3.

Row 5: Yo, k3, yo, p2, (yo, k3, yo, sl1, k2tog, psso, yo, k3, yo, p2,) yo, k3, yo.

Row 6: P5, (k2, p11,) k2, p5.

Row 7: Yo, k3, k2tog, yo, p2, (yo, ssk, k1, k2tog, yo, k1, yo, ssk, k1, k2tog, yo, p2,) yo, ssk, k3, yo.

Row 8: P6, (k2, p11), k2, p6.

Row 9: Yo, k2, (p1, k1) twice, p2, [(k1, p1) twice, k3, (p1, k1) twice, p2,] (k1, p1) twice, k2, yo.

Row 10: P3, (k1, p1) twice, [k2, (p1, k1) twice, p3, (k1, p1) twice,] k2, (p1, k1) twice, p3.

Row 11: Yo, k2, yo, ssk, k1, k2tog, yo, p2, (yo, ssk, k1, k2tog, yo, k1, yo, ssk, k1, k2tog, yo, p2,) yo, ssk, k1, k2tog, yo, k2, yo.

Row 12: P8, (k2, p11,) k2, p8.

Row 13: Yo, k4, (p1, k1) twice, p2, [(k1, p1) twice, k3, (p1, k1) twice, p2,] (k1, p1) twice, k4, yo.

Row 14: P5, (k1, p1) twice, [k2, (p1, k1) twice, p3, (k1, p1) twice,] k2, (p1, k1) twice, p5.

Row 15: Yo, k1, k2tog, yo, k1, yo, ssk, k1, k2tog, yo, p2, (yo, ssk, k1, k2tog, yo, k1, yo, ssk, k1, k2tog, yo, p2,) yo, ssk, k1, k2tog, yo, k1, yo, ssk, k1, yo.

Row 16: P10, (k2, p11,) k2, p10.

Row 17: Yo, p1, k1, p1, k3, (p1, k1) twice, p2, [(k1, p1) twice, k3, (p1, k1) twice, p2,] (k1, p1) twice, k3, p1, k1, p1, yo.

Row 18: (P1, k1) twice, p3, (k1, p1) twice, [k2, (p1, k1) twice, p3, (k1, p1) twice,] k2, (p1, k1) twice, p3, (k1, p1) twice.

Row 19: Yo, k3, k2tog, yo, k1, yo, ssk, k1, k2tog, yo, p2, (yo, ssk, k1, k2tog, yo, k1, yo, ssk, k1, k2tog, yo, p2,) yo, ssk, k1, k2tog, yo, k1, yo, ssk, k3, yo.

Row 20: P12, (k2, p11,) k2, p12.

Row 21: Yo, (p1, k1) twice, p1, k3, (p1, k1) twice, p2, (k1, p1) twice, k3, (p1, k1) twice, p2, (k1, p1) twice, k3, (p1, k1) twice, p1, yo.

Row 22: (P1, k1) three times, p3, (k1, p1) twice, [k2, (p1, k1) twice, p3, (k1,

p1) twice,] k2, (p1, k1) twice, p3, (k1, p1) three times.

wanderlust shawl chart 2: (see page 91)

Row 1 (RS): Yo, p2, (yo, ssk, k1, k2tog, k1, ssk, k1, k2tog, yo, p2) nine times, yo.

Row 2 (WS): P1, (k2, p9 nine times, k2, p1.

Row 3: Yo, k1, yo, p2, (yo, k1, yo, ssk, sk2p, k2tog, yo, k1, yo, p2) nine times, yo, k1, yo.

Row 4: P3, (k2, p9) nine times, k2, p3.

Row 5: Yo, k2tog, yo, k1, yo, p2, (yo, k1, yo, ssk, yo, sk2p, yo, k2tog, yo, k1, yo, p2) nine times, yo, k1, yo, ssk, yo, ssk, yo.

Notes
Shawl is knit from the top down. Begin with a wide stockinette stitch tab into which you will pick up stitches for a 3-stitch stockinette stitch border and the shawl body. Shawl body has four lace sections set off by single spine sts.

INSTRUCTIONS

CO 3 sts.

Beginning with a RS row, work 64 rows in St st.

Next row (RS): K3, do not turn, pick up 63 sts in selvedge, pick up 3 sts in cast-on edge—69 sts.

Set-up row (WS): P3, PM, (p15, PM, p1, PM) three times, p15, PM, p3.

Begin lace pattern
Shawl consists of 3 sts at beg and end to form border, then four sections of 15 sts, divided by single spine sts, all of which are set off by markers. Throughout the pattern, maintain first and last 3 sts and 3 spine sts in St st.

Slip all markers as you come to them, being careful to keep yarn overs on the correct side of stitch markers.

Row 1 & all RS rows: K3, slip marker, (work Chart 1 to marker, sm, k1, sm) three times, work Chart 1 to marker, sm, k3.

Row 2 & all WS rows: P3, sm, (work Chart 1 to marker, sm, p1, sm) three times, work Chart 1 to marker, sm, p3.

Cont to work through Row 22 of chart as established, maintaining first and last 3 sts and single spine sts in St st—173 sts.

Work three more full repeats of Chart 1, repeating highlighted sts on Chart 1 (bracketed in written-out pattern) as needed as sts increase—485 sts.

Next row (RS): K3, sm, (work Chart 2 to marker, sm, k1, sm) three times, work Chart 2 to marker, sm k3.

Row 2 & all WS rows: P3, sm, (work Chart 2 to marker, sm, p1, sm) three times, work Chart 2 to marker, sm, p3.

Cont working through Row 5 of Chart 2 in this manner—525 sts.

BO all sts in pattern loosely.

FINISHING
Weave in all ends and block to measurements.

Wanderlust Shawl Chart 1

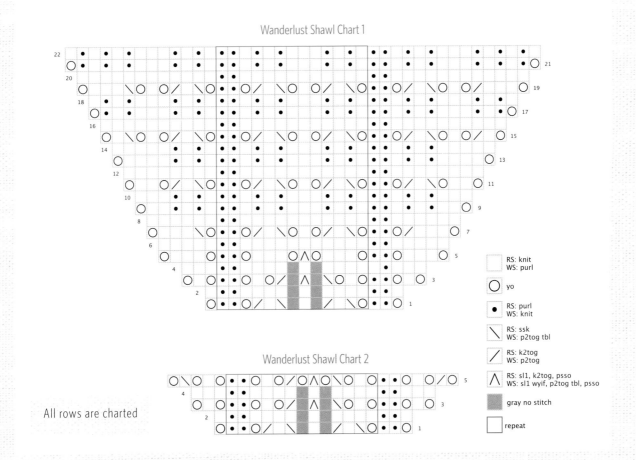

Wanderlust Shawl Chart 2

All rows are charted

□	RS: knit		
	WS: purl		
○	yo		
•	RS: purl		
	WS: knit		
\	RS: ssk		
	WS: p2tog tbl		
/	RS: k2tog		
	WS: p2tog		
∧	RS: sl1, k2tog, psso		
	WS: sl1 wyif, p2tog tbl, psso		
▨	gray no stitch		
□	repeat		

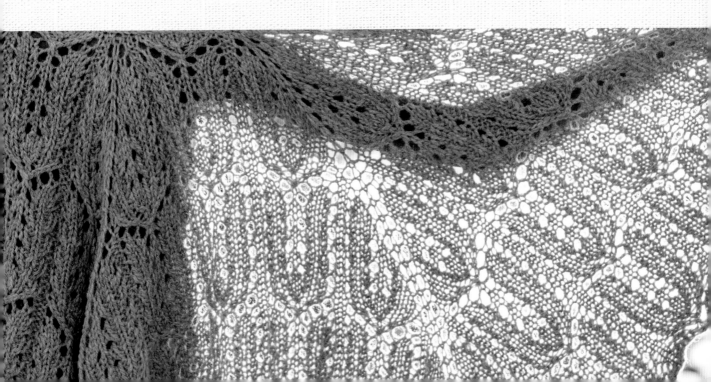

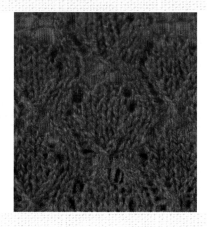

lea sleeveless top

IT'S HARD TO BELIEVE that this cropped top is made from two squares. There is no shaping in the top at all; instead, the drape of the fabric and the open lace motif do all the work. The yarn is held doubled for the yoke section, adding stability and stitch definition to that section. The body pieces are picked up from the yoke and worked down in a simple, easy-to-remember stitch pattern. Personalize yours by knitting to whatever length you prefer, short as pictured here or longer as a tunic.

SKILL LEVEL

INTERMEDIATE

FINISHED MEASUREMENTS

34 (38, 41, 44, 48, 51)"/86 (97, 104, 112, 123, 130)cm to fit bust measurements 32-34 (36-38, 39-41, 42-44, 46-48, 49-51)"

MATERIALS AND TOOLS

Lotus Yarns Tibetan Cloud (100% Tibetan yak; 1.76oz/50g = 490yd/ 450m): 2 (2, 2, 3, 3, 3) skeins, color wine #09—approx 515 (660, 820, 1010, 1150, 1320)/470 (600, 750, 924, 1050, 1200)m of lace weight yarn

Knitting needles: 3.5mm (size U.S. 4) 32" circular needles or size to obtain gauge

3.0mm (size U.S. 2) 24" circular needles or two sizes smaller than above

Spare circ needle or dpn
Tapestry needle
Stitch markers
Coilless safety pins
Stitch holders
Smooth waste yarn

GAUGE

1 repeat of Chart 1 (27 sts and 40 rows) = 3"/8cm wide × 4.5"/11cm tall, using larger needles and 2 strands of yarn held together
1 repeat of Chart 2 (28 sts and 36 rows) = 4"/10cm square, using smaller needles and one strand of yarn
Always take time to check your gauge.

Notes

Lea is knit from the neck down, beginning with the yoke; the yoke is knit flat and grafted to form the tube. Front and back stitches are then picked up along the lower edge of the yoke and worked separately through the armholes. After the armholes are complete, the front and back are rejoined for knitting the lower body in the round.

Yarn is used double-stranded for yoke and single-stranded for front and back.

PATTERN STITCHES

lea sleeveless top chart 1: (see page 96)

Row 1 (RS): K6, yo, ssk, k8, k2tog, yo, k5, yo, ssk, k2—27 sts.

Row 2 AND ALL WS ROWS: P4, yo, p2tog, p15, yo, p2tog, p1, (sl 1 wyif) three times.

Row 3: K6, yo, ssk, k7, k2tog, yo, k6, yo, ssk, k2.

Row 5: K6, yo, ssk, k6, k2tog, yo, k7, yo, ssk, k2.

Row 7: K6, yo, ssk, k5, k2tog, yo, k1, yo, ssk, k5, yo, ssk, k2.

Row 9: K6, yo, ssk, k4, k2tog, yo, k3, yo, ssk, k4, yo, ssk, k2.

Row 11: K6, yo, ssk, k3, k2tog, yo, (k4, yo, ssk) twice, k2.

Row 13: K6, yo, ssk, k2, k2tog, yo, k3, k2tog, yo, k1, yo, ssk, k3, yo, ssk, k2.

Rows 15 & 17: K6, yo, ssk, (k2, k2tog, yo) twice, k3, (yo, ssk, k2) twice.

Row 19: K6, yo, ssk, k2, k2tog, yo, k4, yo, sk2p, yo, k4, yo, ssk, k2.

Row 21: K6, yo, ssk, k4, yo, ssk, k9, yo, ssk, k2.

Row 23: K6, yo, ssk, k5, yo, ssk, k8, yo, ssk, k2.

Row 25: (K6, yo, ssk) twice, k7, yo, ssk, k2.

Row 27: K6, yo, ssk, k4, k2tog, yo, k1, yo, ssk, k6, yo, ssk, k2.

Row 29: K6, yo, ssk, k3, k2tog, yo, k3, yo, ssk, k5, yo, ssk, k2.

Row 31: As Row 11.

Row 33: K6, yo, ssk, k2, k2tog, yo, k1, (yo, ssk, k3) twice, yo, ssk, k2.

Rows 35 & 37: K6, yo, ssk, k1, k2tog, yo, k3, yo, ssk, k2, yo, ssk, k3, yo, ssk, k2.

Row 39: K6, yo, ssk, k3, yo, sk2p, yo, k4, yo, ssk, k3, yo, ssk, k2.

Row 40: P4, yo, p2tog, p15, yo, p2tog, p1, (sl 1 wyif) three times—27 sts.

lea sleeveless top chart 2: (see page 99)

Row 1 (RS): K5, k2tog, k2, yo, k1, *yo, k2, ssk, k3, k2tog, k2, yo, k1, rep from * as needed to last 9 sts, yo, k2, ssk, k2, (sl 1 wyif) three times.

Row 2 and all WS rows: P to last 3 sts, (sl 1 wyif) three times.

Row 3: K4, k2tog, k2, yo, k2, *k1, yo, k2, ssk, k1, k2tog, k2, rep from * as needed to last 9 sts, yo, k2, k, yo, k2, ssk, k, (sl 1 wyif) three times.

Row 5: K3, k2tog, k2, yo, k3, *k2,

yo, k2, sk2p, k2, yo, k3, rep from * as needed to last 9 sts, k2, yo, k2, ssk, (sl 1 wyif) three times.

Row 7: K4, yo, k2, ssk, k2, *k1, k2tog, k2, yo, k1, yo, k2, ssk, k2, rep from * as needed to last 9 sts, k1, k2tog, k2, yo, k1, (sl 1 wyif) three times.

Row 9: K5, yo, k2, ssk, k1, *k2tog, k2, yo, k3, yo, k2, ssk, k1, rep from * to last 9 sts, k2tog, k2, yo, k2, (sl 1 wyif) three times.

Row 11: K6, yo, k2, sk2p, *k2, yo, k5, yo, k2, sk2p, rep from * to last 9 sts, k2, yo, k3, (sl 1 wyif) three times.

Row 12: P to last 3 sts, (sl 1 wyif) three times.

lea sleeveless top chart 3: (see page 99)

Rnd 1: K2, ssk, k1, k2tog, k2, yo, k3, yo—12 sts.

Rnd 2 and all even-numbered rnds: Knit.

Rnd 3: K2, sk2p, k2, yo, k5, yo.

Rnd 5: K2, yo, k1, yo, k2, ssk, k3, k2tog.

Rnd 7: K2, yo, k3, yo, k2, ssk, k1, k2tog.

Rnd 9: K2, yo, k5, yo, k2, sk2p.

Rnd 11: K2, ssk, k3, k2tog, k2, yo, k1, yo.

Rnd 12: Knit—12 sts.

INSTRUCTIONS

yoke

With larger needles and 2 strands of yarn held together, CO 27 sts using waste yarn and provisional cast-on method.

Work 7 (7, 8, 8, 9, 9) full repeats of Chart 1.

Remove waste yarn from provisional cast on and transfer live sts to spare needle. Graft seam.

set-up for body

Hold yoke with RS facing and longer yoke edge at the top; selvedge edge with slipped sts will be slightly shorter and forms neck edge of yoke.

Place coilless safety pins along longer yoke edge as follows: Place first pin (marker A) at graft seam; place second pin (marker B) 8½ (8½, 9½, 9½, 10½, 10½)"/22 (22, 24, 24, 27, 27)cm from first marker; place third pin (marker C) 7½ (7½, 8½, 8½, 9½, 9½)"/19 (19, 22, 22, 24, 24)cm from second marker; place fourth pin (marker D) 8½ (8½, 9½, 9½, 10½, 10½)"/22 (22, 24, 24, 27, 27)cm from third marker.

back

With smaller needle and one strand of yarn, pick up and knit 61 (67, 73, 79, 85, 91) sts between markers A and B. Turn.

Set up row (WS): P4, *yo, p1, rep from * to last 3 sts, p3—115 (127, 139, 151, 163, 175) sts.

Work Rows 1–12 of Chart 2 a total of 2 (2, 3, 3, 4, 4) times, then work rows 1–11 once.

Next row (WS): Sl first 3 sts to waste yarn, p to last 3 sts; sl these 3 sts to dpn and work 11 rows of I-cord over these 3 sts only. ** Place these 3 sts on waste yarn. Slip rem 109 (121, 133, 145, 157, 169) sts to holder for lower back.

front

With smaller needle and one strand of yarn, pick up and knit 61, (67, 73, 79, 85, 91) sts between markers C and D. Turn.

Work as for back to ** and then graft 3-stitch I-cord at each underarm.

join for lower body

Note

To create lower body, work across front sts, pick up sts across underarm, work across back sts, pick up first portion of sts for underarm, place marker to show beg of rnd, pick up rem sts for underarm.

Return front 109 (121, 133, 145, 157, 169) sts to needle and work as follows: *(K2, k2tog, k2, yo, k1, yo, k2, ssk, k1), rep from * to last front st., k1; now pick up and knit 11 sts across underarm I-cord; return back 109 (121, 133, 145, 157, 169) sts to needle and work as for front; pick up and knit 8 sts across half of underarm I-cord; place marker to show beg of rnd; pick up and knit 3 rem sts across underarm—240 (264, 288, 312, 336, 360) sts.

Knit 1 rnd.

Work rows 1–12 of Chart 3 a total of 8 (8, 9, 9, 10, 10) times or until body is desired length.

BO all sts loosely knitwise.

FINISHING

Weave in all ends. Block piece to measurements.

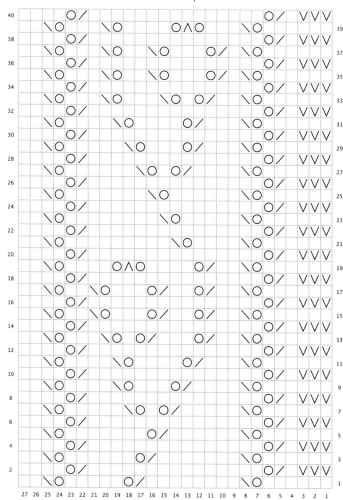

Lea Sleeveless Top Chart 1

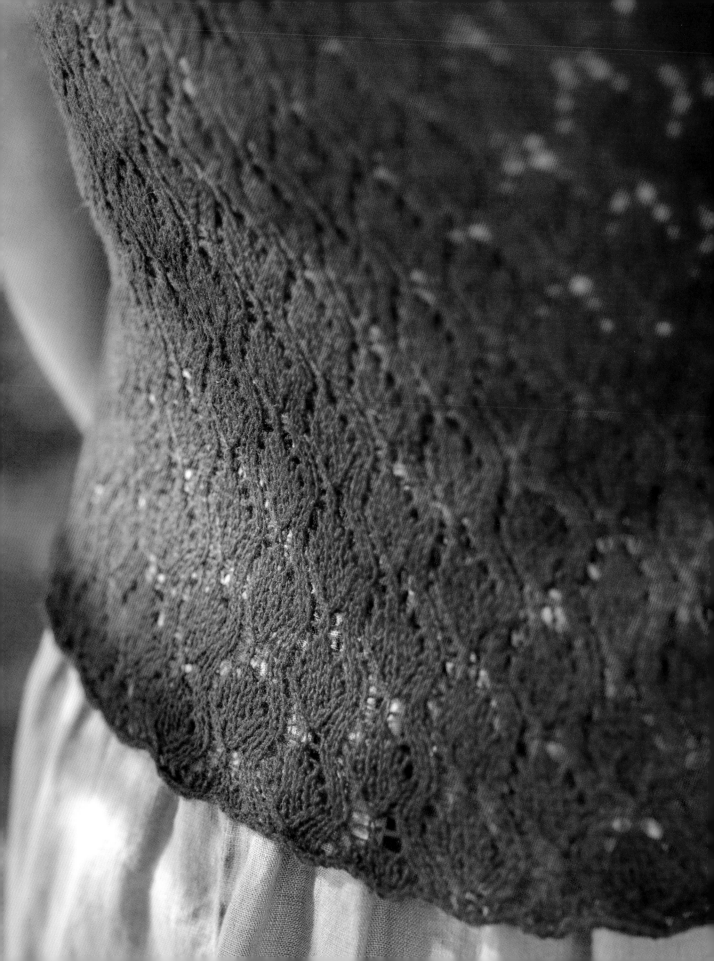

Lea Sleeveless Top Chart 2

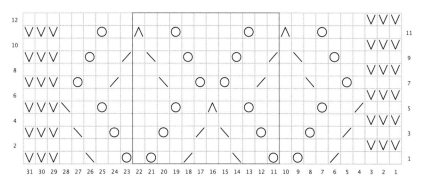

Lea Sleeveless Top Chart 3

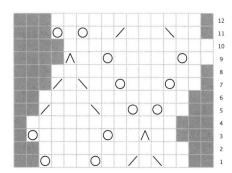

	RS: knit WS: purl
O	yo
/	RS: k2tog WS: p2tog
\	RS: ssk WS: p2tog tbl
∧	RS: sl1, k2tog, psso WS: sl1 wyif, p2tog tbl, psso
V	RS: slip WS: slip purlwise with yarn in front
▨	gray no stitch

All rows are charted

Lea Sleeveless Top Schematic

8.5 (8.5, 9.5, 9.5, 10.5, 10.5)"

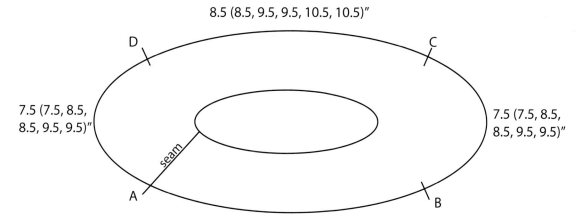

7.5 (7.5, 8.5, 8.5, 9.5, 9.5)"

7.5 (7.5, 8.5, 8.5, 9.5, 9.5)"

8.5 (8.5, 9.5, 9.5, 10.5, 10.5)"

rectangles

EVERY BEGINNER KNITTER starts by making rectangles that usually become scarves. Knit either lengthwise or widthwise, the rectangle is an easy shape to knit and design with little or minimal shaping. In this chapter, however, we're going to take those rectangles to the next level and create a variety of accessories and garments!

uno cowl

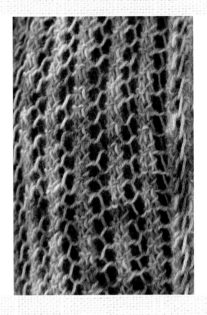

A SIMPLE ONE-ROW STITCH PATTERN is a great way to try your hand at lace on both sides. Fagot patterns are vertical stitch patterns with columns of eyelets or yarn overs alternating with columns of decreases. These mesh patterns with lace on every row are remarkably stable in spite of their openness, because each eyelet is knit on the return row. In this fagot pattern, remember that the second knit stitch in each repeat should be worked into the yarn over from the row below. This will help keep you on track and allow you to catch simple mistakes such as a dropped yarn over immediately.

I've chosen to work this in a lace weight yarn because of its delicate nature. However, this cowl can be worked in any yarn at any gauge. The cowl shown in the inset photo on page 102 is worked in a bulky yarn with a U.S size 19 needle over 16 stitches. Just cast on a multiple of four stitches and work as indicated with your favorite yarn to create your own cowl or scarf.

SKILL LEVEL

EASY

FINISHED MEASUREMENTS

Approx 8"/20cm wide × 63½"/161cm long after blocking

MATERIALS AND TOOLS

Black Bunny Fibers Oakwood (36% angora, 30% merino, 26% tencel, 8% cashmere; 50g = 390yd/357m): 1 skein, color violetta—approx 375yd/343m of lace weight yarn

Knitting needles: 3.25mm (size 3 U.S.) or size to obtain gauge

Tapestry needle

Tapestry needle

GAUGE

28 sts/40 rows = 4"/10cm after blocking
Always take time to check your gauge.

PATTERN STITCHES

Fagot pattern (mult of 4 sts)

Row 1: K3, *yo, k2tog, k2, rep from * to last st, k1.

Rep this row for patt.

INSTRUCTIONS

CO 56 sts.

Begin working Fagot patt and cont until piece measures 60"/152cm.

BO all sts.

FINISHING

Weave in ends and block.

Sew cast-on edge to bound-off edge, twisting piece once, to form cowl.

Note
Piece may be left unseamed and worn as a scarf.

primrose tunic

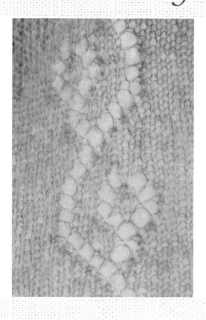

A FLOWERING LACE MOTIF meanders up the panels of this long tunic. The panels are knit separately and feature an easy-to-remember pattern, making this a great take-along project. If the thought of making an entire dress intimidates you, think of it as knitting scarves—or, if you choose, make just a scarf by knitting only one of the panels. Simple short-row shaping in each of the panels creates the elegant A-line shape of the tunic, and the lovely mohair/silk blend gives it an ethereal quality.

SKILL LEVEL

INTERMEDIATE

FINISHED MEASUREMENTS

Bust 42 (47, 52)"/107 (119, 132)cm
To fit bust measurement 36–40
(42–45, 46–50)"

MATERIALS AND TOOLS

KFI/Debbie Bliss Angel (76% superfine kid mohair, 24% silk; .88oz/25g
= 220yd/201m): (A) 2 (2, 2) skeins,
color mint #15011; (B) 2 (2, 3)
skeins, color lime #15012; (C) 2 (2,
3) skeins, color jade #15010—approx
1150 (1300, 1500)yd/1052 (1189,
1372)m of lace weight yarn

Knitting needles: 3.75mm (size 5
U.S.) or size to obtain gauge

4mm (size G U.S.) crochet hook

Stitch markers

GAUGE

20 sts/32 rows = 4"/10cm over St st after blocking
Always take time to check your gauge.

PATTERN STITCHES

Primrose Tunic Lace Chart (over 12 sts): (see page 111)

Row 27: K3, k2tog, yo, k1, yo, ssk, k4.

Row 29: K2, k2tog, yo, k3, yo, ssk, k3.

Row 31: K2, k2tog, yo, k4, yo, ssk, k2.

Row 33: K1, k2tog, yo, k1, yo, ssk, k3, yo, ssk, k1.

Rows 35 & 37: K2tog, yo, k3, yo, ssk, k2, yo, ssk, k1.

Row 39: K2, yo, sk2p, yo, k4, yo, ssk, k1.

Row 40: Purl.

INSTRUCTIONS

Note
The tunic is knit in several wedge-shaped panels (see schematic), working from the bottom up and using short-row shaping. Because the panels vary in height, note carefully the number of lace pattern repeats each panel requires. Yarn color alternates from panel to panel. Individual panels are blocked and then seamed.

You may have seen references to "fully fashioned shaping" in knitting patterns, or you may have wondered exactly how to work decreases when they are not specified in the text of the pattern. For each panel of the Primrose Tunic, I recommend that you work a left-leaning decrease at the beginning of the decrease rows and then a right-leaning decrease at the end of the decrease rows. In other words, work decrease rows in the Primrose Tunic like this: "K1, ssk, k to marker, work next row of Chart 1, knit to last 3 sts, k2tog, k1." The left-leaning ssk and the right-leaning k2tog are symmetric and will give the finished garment a very professional look, especially after blocking.

together. After seaming, neck and armhole bands are crocheted on. You may wish to label panels as they are worked to make assembly easier.

panel 1

Note: Panel 1 begins at the hem and ends at the left underarm.

With A, CO 30 (32, 34) sts.

Set-up rows:

Row 1 (RS): Purl.

Row 2 & all WS rows: Purl.

Row 3: K6 (7, 8), w&t.

Row 5: K12 (13, 14), w&t.

Row 7: K18 (19, 20), w&t.

Row 9: K24 (25, 26), w&t.

Row 11: K9 (10, 11), place marker, k12, PM, k9 (10, 11).

Row 12: Purl.

Begin lace pattern:
Next row (RS): K9 (10, 11), slip marker, work Chart 1 to next marker, sm, k9 (10, 11).

Row 2 (WS): Purl.

Cont as established, maintaining first and last sts in St st and working through sequential rows of Chart 1

until you have worked Chart 1 a total of four times and at the same time decr 1 st at each end of 21s and each subsequent 20th row—a total of 7 decr rows worked; 16 (18, 20) sts rem after all decr rows worked.

After working last WS row of last repeat of Chart 1, BO all sts loosely knitwise.

panel 2

Note: Panel 2 begins at the hem and ends at the back left shoulder.

With B, CO 36 (38, 40) sts.

Set-up rows:

Row 1 (RS): Purl.

Row 2 & all WS rows: Purl.

Row 3: K6 (7, 8), w&t.

Row 3: K6 (7, 8) w&t.

Row 5: K12 (13, 14), w&t.

Row 7: K18 (19, 20), w&t.

Row 9: K24 (25, 26), w&t.

Row 11: K30 (31, 32), w&t.

Row 13: K12 (13, 14), pm, k12, pm, k12 (13, 14).

Row 14: Purl.

Begin lace pattern:
Work lace patt as for Panel 1, maintaining first and last sts in St st and working through sequential rows of Chart 1 using 12 sts between markers until you have worked Chart 1 a total of five times, then work the first 20 rows of Chart 1 once more and at the same time decr 1 st at each end of 21st and each subsequent 20th row—a total of 10 decr rows worked; 16 (28, 20) sts rem after all decr rows worked.

After working last WS row of last repeat of Chart 1, BO all sts loosely knitwise.

panel 3

Note: Panel 3 begins at the hem and ends at the left back neck.

With CO 30 (32, 34) sts.

Work Set-up rows 1–12 as for Panel 1.

Begin lace pattern:
Next row (RS): K9 (10, 11), slip marker, work Chart 1 to next marker, sm, k9 (10, 11).

Row 2 (WS): Purl.

Cont as established, maintaining first and last sts in St st and working through sequential rows of Chart 1 until you have worked one full repeat of Chart 1 without decreasing.

Now work three more repeats of Chart 1 in the same manner and at the same time decr 1 st at each end of 1st and each subsequent 20th row—6 decr rows worked; 18 (20, 22) sts rem after all decr rows worked.

Work the first 20 rows of Chart 1 in the same manner, decr on the first row only—16 (18, 20) sts rem.*

Next row (RS): K1, ssk, k2 (3, 4), yo, ssk, k6 (7, 8), k2tog, k1—14 (16, 18) sts.

Row 2 & ALL WS ROWS: Purl.

Row 3: K5 (6, 7), yo, ssk, k7 (8, 9).

Row 5: K6 (7, 8), yo, ssk, k6 (7, 8).

Row 7: K1, ssk, k4 (5, 6), yo, ssk, k2 (3, 4), k2tog, k1—12 (14, 16) sts.

Row 9: K7 (8, 9), yo, ssk, k3 (4, 5).

Row 11: K8 (9, 10), yo, ssk, k2 (3, 4).

Row 12: Purl.

BO all sts loosely knitwise.

panel 4

NOTE: Panel 4 begins at the hem and ends at the center back neck.

With A, CO 30 (32, 34) sts.

Work Set-up rows as for Panel 1.

Begin lace pattern:
Work the same as lace pattern of Panel 3 to *—16 (18, 20) sts rem.

NEXT ROW (RS): K1 (2, 3), move marker, ssk, k2, yo, ssk, k6, k2tog, move marker, k1 (2, 3)—14 (16, 18) sts. Note: First ssk and k2tog each require use of 1 st on either side of marker; move 1st marker so that it sits before ssk and 2nd marker so that it sits after k2tog.

Row 2 (WS): Purl.

Rows 3–19: K1, work rows 23–39 of Chart 1 between markers, k1.

Row 20: Purl.

BO all sts loosely knitwise.

panel 5

NOTE: Panel 5 begins at the hem and ends at the right back neck.

With B, CO 30 (32, 34) sts.

Work the same as Panel 4 through Row 20 of Chart 2. Do not bind off,

but continue as follows:

NEXT ROW (RS): K1, ssk, k5 (6, 7), k2tog, yo, k1 (2, 3), k2tog, k1—12 (14, 16) sts.

Row 2 & ALL WS ROWS: Purl.

Row 3: K6 (7, 8), k2tog, yo, k4 (5, 6).

Row 5: K5 (6, 7), k2tog, yo, k5 (6, 7).

Row 7: K4 (5, 6), k2tog, yo, k6 (7, 8).

Row 8: Purl.

BO all sts loosely knitwise.

panel 6

NOTE: Panel 6 begins at the hem and ends at the right back shoulder.

With C, CO 36 (38, 40) sts.

Work Rows 1–14 of Panel 2.

Begin lace pattern:
NEXT ROW (RS): K to marker, sm, work Chart 1 to next marker, sm, k to end.

Row 2 (WS): Purl.

Cont as established, maintaining first and last sts in St st and working through sequential rows of Chart 1 until you have worked one full repeat of Chart 1 without decreasing. Work first 20 rows of Chart 1 again without decreasing. Work rem 20 rows of Chart 1, decr 1 st at each end of next row—34 (36, 38) sts rem. Now work four more full repeats of Chart 1 and at the same time decr 1 st at each end of 1st and each subsequent 20th row—8 dec rows worked; 18 (20, 22) sts rem.

Work the first 6 rows of Chart 1 in the same manner, decr on the first row only—16 (18, 20) sts rem.

NEXT ROW (RS): K to marker, sm, k4, k2tog, yo, k5, sm, k to end.

Row 2 & ALL WS ROWS: Purl.

Row 3: K to marker, sm, k3, k2tog, yo, k7, sm, k to end.

Row 5: K to marker, k2, k2tog, yo, k8, sm, k to end.

Row 7: K to marker, k1, k2tog, yo, k9, sm, k to end.

Row 8: Purl.

BO all sts loosely knitwise.

panel 7

NOTE: Panel 7 begins at the hem and ends at the right underarm.

With A, CO 30 (32, 34) sts.

SET-UP ROWS:

Row 1 (RS): Purl.

Row 2 (WS): P6 (7, 8), w&t.

Rows 3, 5, 7, & 9: Knit.

Row 4: P12 (13, 14), w&t.

Row 6: P18 (19, 20), w&t.

Row 8: P24 (25, 26), w&t.

Row 10: P9 (10, 11), PM, k12, PM, p9 (10, 11).

Begin lace pattern:
NEXT ROW (RS): Sl 1, k to marker, sm, work Chart 1 to next marker, sm, k to end.

Row 2 (WS): Purl.

Cont as established, maintaining first and last sts in St st and working through sequential rows of Chart 1 until you have worked two full repeats of Chart 1 without decreasing. Now work three more full repeats of Chart 1 and at the same time decr 1 st at each end of 1st and each subsequent 20th row—total of 6 dec rows worked; 18 (20, 22) sts rem. Work the first 6 rows of Chart 1 in the same manner, decr on the first row only—16 (18, 20) sts rem.

NEXT ROW (RS): K to m, sm, k4, k2tog, yo, k6, sm, k to end.

Row 2 (WS): Purl.

Row 3: K to m, sm, k3, ktog, yo, k7, sm, k to end.

Row 4: Purl.

BO all sts loosely knitwise.

panel 8

NOTE: Panel 8 begins at hem and ends at right front shoulder.

With B, CO 36 (38, 40) sts.

SET-UP ROWS:

Row 1 (RS): Purl.

Row 2 (WS): P6 (7, 8), w&t.

Rows 3, 5, 7, 9, & 11: Sl 1, k to end.

Row 4: P12 (13, 14), w&t.

Row 6: P18 (19, 20), w&t.

Row 8: P24 (25, 26), w&t.

Row 10: P30 (31, 32), w&t.

Row 12: P12 (13, 14), PM, p12, PM, p12 (13, 14).

Begin lace pattern:
Work as for lace pattern of Panel 6 through BO.

panel 9

NOTE: Panel 9 begins at the hem and ends at the right front neck.

With C, CO 30 (32, 34) sts.

SET-UP ROWS:

Work as for Set-up rows of Panel 7.

Begin lace pattern:
Work as for lace pattern of Panel 4 through Row 20; do not BO. Cont as follows:

*Row 1 (RS):** K1 (2, 3), sm, work Row 1 of chart, k1 (2, 3).

Row 2 & all WS rows: P.

Rows 3, 5, 7, & 9: K1 (2, 3), sm, work next sequential row of chart, k1 (2, 3), removing markers on last row.

Row 11: K1, ssk, k1 (2, 3), yo, ssk, k5 (6, 7), k2tog, k1—12, 14, 16 sts.

Row 13: K4 (5, 6), yo, ssk, k6 (7, 8).

Row 15: K5 (6, 7), yo, ssk, k5 (6, 7).

Row 17: K6 (7, 8), yo, ssk, k4 (5, 6).

Row 19: K7 (8, 9), yo, ssk, k3 (4, 5).

Row 21: K8 (9, 10), yo, ssk, k2 (3, 4).

Row 22: Purl.

BO all sts loosely knitwise.

panel 10

NOTE: Panel 10 begins at the hem and ends at the center front neck.

With A, CO 30 (32, 34) sts.

Work Set-up rows as for Panel 7.

Begin lace pattern:
Work lace pattern as for Panel 4, ending with Row 20; do not BO.

Now work Rows 1–20 as for lace pattern of Panel 9 (begin at *).

Cont as follows:

Row 21 (RS): K1, ssk, k1 (2, 3), yo, ssk, k5 (6, 7), k2tog, k1—12 (14, 16) sts.

Row 22 (WS): Purl.

Row 23: K4 (5, 6), yo, ssk, k6 (7, 8).

Row 24: Purl.

BO all sts loosely knitwise.

panel 11

NOTE: Panel 11 begins at the hem and ends at the left front neck.

With B, CO 30 (32, 34) sts.

Work Set-up rows as for Panel 7.

Begin lace pattern:
Work lace pattern as for Panel 4, ending with Row 20; do not BO.

Now work Rows 1–20 as for lace pattern of Panel 9 (begin at *).

Cont as follows:

Row 21: K1, ssk, k5 (6, 7), k2tog, yo, k1 (2, 3), k2tog, k1—12 (14, 16) sts.

Row 23: K6 (7, 8), k2tog, yo, k4 (5, 6).

Row 25: K5 (6, 7), k2tog, yo, k5 (6, 7).

Row 27: K4(5, 6), k2tog, yo, k6 (7, 8).

Row 29: K3 (4, 5), k2tog, yo, k7 (8, 9).

Row 21: K2 (3, 4), k2tog, yo, k8 (9, 10).

Row 23: K4 (5, 6), yo, ssk, k6 (7, 8).

Row 25: K5 (6, 7), yo, ssk, k5 (6, 7).

Row 27: K6 (7, 8), yo, ssk, k4 (5, 6)—12 (14, 16) sts.

Row 29: BO all sts loosely knitwise.

panel 12

NOTE: Panel 12 begins at the hem and ends at the left front shoulder.

With C, CO 36 (38, 40) sts.

Work Set-up rows as for Panel 8.

Begin lace pattern:
Work as for lace pattern of Panel 6 through BO.

FINISHING

Block panels.

Sew panels together, following schematic for placement and matching panels at hem line.

Sew shoulder seams. Weave in all ends.

Neckband:
With RS facing and yarn A, work 1 row of sc around neck edge.

Armhole facing:
With RS facing and yarn A, work 1 row of sc around neck edge.

Primrose Tunic Chart

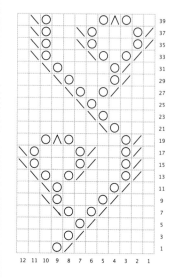

	RS: knit WS: purl
O	yo
/	RS: k2tog WS: p2tog
\	RS: ssk WS: p2tog tbl
∧	RS: sl1, k2tog, psso WS: sl1 wyif, p2tog tbl, psso

Primrose Tunic Schematic

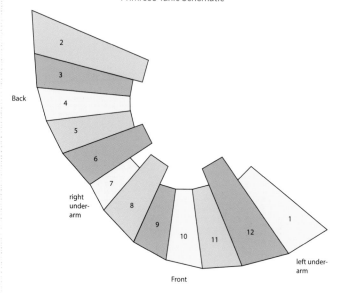

Only odd-numbered rows are charted; all even-numbered rows are purl across.

troika wrap

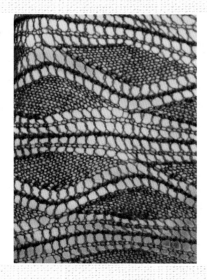

IN NINETEENTH-CENTURY RUSSIA, the nobility traveled in a carriage drawn by a team of three horses that was called a troika. This simple rectangular piece with cleverly placed buttons can be worn in three ways: as a stole, a shrug, or a poncho. Each way offers simple luxury and comfort thanks to the truly heavenly fiber from Buffalo Wool Company.

SKILL LEVEL

◖◼◼◼◻
INTERMEDIATE

FINISHED MEASUREMENTS

53"/135cm wide by 17"/43cm tall

MATERIALS AND TOOLS

Buffalo Wool Company Heaven (100% bison; 1.76oz/50g = 400yd/366m): 1 skein, color natural—approx 400yd/ 366m of lace weight yarn 🧶

Knitting needles: 3.5mm (size 4 U.S.) needle or size to obtain gauge

Stitch markers

Twelve buttons, ⅝"/16mm diameter

GAUGE

1 repeat of highlighted section in chart (38 sts/36 rows) = 7 3/4"/20cm wide × 5"/13cm tall after blocking
Always take time to check your gauge.

PATTERN STITCHES

troika wrap lace chart: (see page 117)

Row 1 (RS): K2, *k1, yo, sk2p, (yo, k1) twice, yo, sk2p, yo, ssk, k6, ssk, yo, k1, yo, sk2p, yo, k1, yo, k2tog, k6, k2tog, yo, sk2p, yo, k1, yo, rep from * once more, k1, yo, sk2p, yo, k3.

Row 2 AND ALL WS ROWS: P.

Row 3: K2, *k1, yo, sk2p, yo, k1, yo, k2, yo, sk2p, yo, ssk, k5, ssk, yo, k1, yo, sk2p, yo, k1, yo, k2tog, k5, k2tog, yo, sk2p, yo, k2, yo, rep from * once more, k1, yo, sk2p, yo, k3.

Row 5: K2, *k1, yo, sk2p, yo, k1, yo, k3, yo, sk2p, yo, ssk, k4, ssk, yo, k1, yo, sk2p, yo, k1, yo, k2tog, k4, k2tog, yo, sk2p, yo, k3, yo, rep from * once more, k1, yo, sk2p, yo, k3.

Row 7: K2, *k1, yo, sk2p, yo, k1, yo, k4, yo, sk2p, yo, ssk, k3, ssk, yo, k1, yo, sk2p, yo, k1, yo, k2tog, k3, k2tog, yo, sk2p, yo, k4, yo, rep from * once more, k1, yo, sk2p, yo, k3.

Row 9: K2, *k1, yo, sk2p, yo, k1, yo, k5, yo, sk2p, yo, ssk, k2, ssk, yo, k1, yo, sk2p, yo, k1, yo, k2tog, k2, k2tog, yo, sk2p, yo, k5, yo, rep from * once more, k1, yo, sk2p, yo, k3.

Row 11: K2, *k1, yo, sk2p, yo, k1, yo, k6, yo, sk2p, yo, ssk, k1, ssk, yo, k1, yo, sk2p, yo, k1, yo, k2tog, k1, k2tog, yo, sk2p, yo, k6, yo, rep from * once more, k1, yo, sk2p, yo, k3.

Row 13: K2, *k1, yo, sk2p, yo, k1, yo, k7, yo, sk2p, yo, ssk twice, yo, k1, yo, sk2p, yo, k1, yo, k2tog twice, yo, sk2p, yo, k7, yo, rep from * once more, k1, yo, sk2p, yo, k3.

Row 15: K2, *k1, yo, sk2p, yo, k1, yo, k8, yo, sk2p, (yo, sk2p, yo, k) twice, (yo, sk2p) twice, yo, k8, yo, rep from * once more, k1, yo, sk2p, yo, k3.

Row 17: K2, *k1, yo, sk2p, yo, k1, yo, k9, yo, sk2p, yo, ssk, yo, sk2p, yo, k1, k2tog, yo, sk2p, yo, k9, yo, rep from * once more, k1, yo, sk2p, yo, k3.

Row 19: K2, *k1, yo, sk2p, yo, k1, yo, k2tog, k6, k2tog, [yo, sk2p, (yo, k1) twice] twice, yo, sk2p, yo, ssk, k6, ssk, yo, rep from * once more, k1, yo, sk2p, yo, k3.

Row 21: K2, *k1, yo, sk2p, yo, k1, yo, k2tog, k5, k2tog, yo, sk2p, yo, k2, yo, k1, yo, sk2p, yo, k1, yo, k2, yo, sk2p, yo, ssk, k5, ssk, yo, rep from * once more, k1, yo, sk2p, yo, k3.

Row 23: K2, *k1, yo, sk2p, yo, k1, yo, k2tog, k4, k2tog, yo, sk2p, yo, k3, yo, k1, yo, sk2p, yo, k1, yo, k3, yo, sk2p, yo, ssk, k4, ssk, yo, rep from * once more, k1, yo, sk2p, yo, k3.

Row 25: K2, *k1, yo, sk2p, yo, k1, yo, k2tog, k3, k2tog, yo, sk2p, yo, k4, yo, k1, yo, sk2p, yo, k1, yo, k4, yo, sk2p, yo, ssk, k3, ssk, yo, rep from * once more, k1, yo, sk2p, yo, k3.

Row 27: K2, *k1, yo, sk2p, yo, k1, yo, k2tog, k2, k2tog, yo, sk2p, yo, k5, yo, k1, yo, sk2p, yo, k1, yo, k5, yo, sk2p, yo, ssk, k2, ssk, yo, rep from * once more, k1, yo, sk2p, yo, k3.

Row 29: K2, *k1, yo, sk2p, yo, k1, yo, k2tog, k1, k2tog, yo, sk2p, yo, k6, yo, k1, yo, sk2p, yo, k1, yo, k6, yo, sk2p, yo, ssk, k1, ssk, yo, rep from * once more, k1, yo, sk2p, yo, k3.

Row 31: K2, *k1, yo, sk2p, yo, k1, yo, k2tog twice, yo, sk2p, yo, k7, yo, k1, yo, sk2p, yo, k1, yo, k7, yo, sk2p, yo, ssk twice, yo, rep from * once more, k1, yo, sk2p, yo, k3.

Row 33: K2, *(k1, yo, sk2p, yo) twice, sk2p, yo, k8, yo, k1, yo, sk2p, yo, k1, yo, k8, (yo, sk2p) twice, yo, rep from * once more, k1, yo, sk2p, yo, k3.

Row 35: K2, *k1, yo, sk2p, yo, k1, k2tog, yo, sk2p, yo, k9, yo, k1, yo, sk2p, yo, k1, yo, k9, yo, sk2p, yo, ssk, rep from * once more, k1, yo, sk2p, yo, k3.

Row 36: P.

INSTRUCTIONS

Note
Garment is knitted sideways, from cuff to cuff. Use Troika Lace Chart (or written-out directions) for body section; only RS rows are charted—all WS rows are purled across.

CO 57 sts.

right cuff

Row 1 (RS): K3, *yo, sk2p, yo, (k1, p1) four times, k1, rep from * to last 6 sts, yo, sk2p, yo, k3.

Row 2 (WS): P7, *(k1, p1) four times, p4, rep from * to last 2 sts, p2.

Rows 3–10: Rep Rows 1 and 2 four more times.

Row 11 (RS): K3, *yo, sk2p, yo, k1, (kf&b) seven times, k1, rep from * to last 6 sts, yo, sk2p, yo, k3—85 sts.

Row 12: Purl.

body

NEXT ROW & ALL RS ROWS: Work chart, working highlighted stitches on charts twice in each row or use written instructions above.

Row 2 & ALL WS ROWS: Purl.

Cont to work through Row 36 of chart, then rep these 36 rows nine more times (work a total of ten repeats of chart)—85 sts.

left cuff

Discontinue chart and work as follows:

Row 1 (RS): K3, *yo, sk2p, yo, k16, rep from * to last 6 sts, yo, sk2p, yo, k3.

Row 2 (WS): P7, *(p2tog) seven times, p5, rep from * to last 2 sts, p2—57 sts.

Row 3: K3, *yo, sk2p, yo, (k1, p1) four times, k1, rep from * to last 6 sts, yo, sk2p, yo, k3.

Row 4: P7, *(k1, p1) four times, p4, rep from * to last 2 sts, p2.

Rows 5–12: Rep Rows 3 and 4 four times more.

BO all sts loosely in pattern.

FINISHING
Weave in all ends. Block piece to measurements.

Lay out rectangle with long sides at top and bottom. Beginning at cast-on edge (upper right corner of rectangle), sew 6 buttons, spaced 3.5"/9cm apart, along top long edge, ending approx. 18½"/47cm from corner. Attach six buttons to bottom long edge, beg at lower left corner of rectangle. Buttons fasten by slipping through eyelets of lace pattern.

Troika Wrap Lace Chart

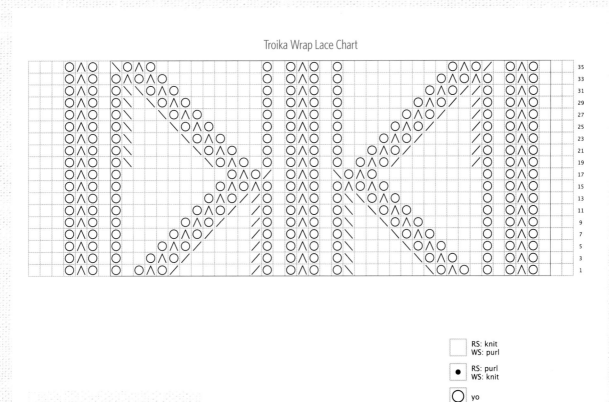

Only odd-numbered rows are charted; all even-numbered rows are purl across.

	RS: knit
	WS: purl
●	RS: purl
	WS: knit
◯	yo
⋀	RS: sl1, k2tog, psso
	WS: sl1 wyif, p2tog tbl, psso
⟍	RS: ssk
	WS: p2tog tbl
⟋	RS: k2tog
	WS: p2tog
	repeat

Troika Wrap Schematic

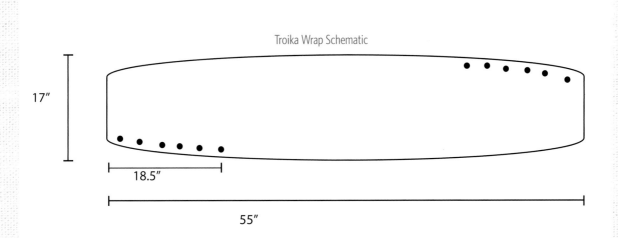

17"

18.5"

55"

duo vest

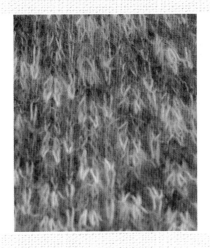

IN THIS VEST, WE'RE TAKING OUR SKILLS in the fagot stitch to the next level. As in Uno, we're working a vertical mesh pattern, with columns of yarn overs and decreases. However, this is a two-row pattern, with the wrong-side rows all purled across. After the wrong-side rows are purled, the eyelets are separated by a pair of twisted strands, resulting in a firm, stable fabric suitable for a garment. The vertical columns of decreases frame the eyelets, forcing the holes to bloom and remain open even as the fabric drapes.

To take advantage of the flow of this fagot pattern, I created this vest with a surplice drape front opening. The vibrant colors of this handpaint yarn can shine in the simple lace motif rather than fighting against a more complicated lace pattern.

SKILL LEVEL

INTERMEDIATE

FINISHED MEASUREMENTS

Chest 40 (44, 48, 52)"/102 (112, 122, 132)cm
To fit bust measurement 36-38 (40-42, 44-46, 48-50)"

MATERIALS AND TOOLS

Black Bunny Fibers Cumulus (70% superfine kid mohair, 30% silk; 1.75oz/50g = 450yd/411m): 2 (2, 3, 3) skeins, color Fluffykins—approx 700 (850, 1000, 1200) yd/640 (777, 914, 1097)m of lace weight yarn

Knitting needles: 3.75mm (size 5 U.S.), 47" circular needles or size to obtain gauge

3.25mm (size 3 U.S.), 24" circular needles or two sizes smaller than above

Tapestry needle

GAUGE

21 sts/24 rows = 4"/10cm using larger needle after blocking
Always take time to check your gauge.

PATTERN STITCHES

Fagot pattern (mult of 5 + 2):

Row 1 (RS): K1, *k2tog, yo, k1, yo, ssk, rep from * to last st, k1.

Row 2 (WS): P.

Rep Rows 1 & 2 for patt.

Note
Vest is worked in one piece from the bottom to the armholes; then left front, right front, and back are each worked separately.

INSTRUCTIONS

body

Using larger needle, CO 287 (307, 327, 347) sts.

Work in fagot patt until piece measures 10"/25cm from cast-on edge.

Work armholes
NEXT ROW (RS): K1, (k2tog, yo, k1, yo, ssk) 17 (18, 19, 20) times, k1, BO next 8 sts for armhole, (k2tog, yo, k1, yo, ssk) 19 (21, 23, 25) times, k1, BO next 8 sts for second armhole, (k2tog, yo, k1, yo, ssk) 17 (18, 19, 20) times, k1—271 (291, 311, 331) sts rem.

Divide for fronts and back:
NEXT ROW: P87 (92, 97, 102) sts for left front, sl next 97 (107, 117, 127) sts to holder for back, sl next 87 (92, 97, 102) sts to holder for right front.

left front

Working back and forth on 87 (92, 97, 102) left front sts only and beg with a RS row, cont working fagot patt as established (maintaining first and last st in St st) until piece measures 9 (9, 10, 10)"/23 (23, 25, 25)cm from bound-off underarm sts, ending with a WS row.

Shape front
NEXT ROW (RS): K1, (k2tog, k1, ssk) 5 (5, 6, 6) times, (k2tog, yo, k1, yo, ssk) 12 (13, 13, 14) times, k1—77 (82, 85, 90) sts.

NEXT ROW (WS): P.

NEXT ROW (RS): BO first 15 (15, 18, 18) sts, *k2tog, yo, k1 yo, ssk, rep from * to last st, k1—62(67, 67, 72) sts.

Work left collar
Work 56 (58, 60, 62) more rows of fagot patt (maintaining first and last sts in St st), ending with a WS row.

NEXT ROW (RS): K1, *k2tog, k1, ssk, rep from * to last st, k1—38 (41, 41, 44) sts.

Break yarn. Place rem 38 (41, 41, 44) sts on holder; these will be grafted to corresponding sts from right front to form collar.

right front

Transfer 87 (92, 97, 102) sts for right front from holder to needle. With WS facing, rejoin yarn and purl 1 row. Beg with a RS row, cont working in fagot st patt as established (maintaining first

and last st in St st) until right front measures 9 (9, 10, 10)"/23 (23, 25, 25)cm from bound-off underarm sts, ending with a WS row.

Shape front
NEXT ROW (RS): K1, (k2tog, yo, k1, yo, ssk) 12 (13, 13, 14) times, (k2tog, k1, ssk) 5 (5, 6, 6) times, k1—77 (82, 85, 90) sts.

NEXT ROW (WS): BO first 15 (15, 18, 18) sts purlwise, p to end of row—62 (67, 67, 72) sts.

Work right collar
Work 56 (58, 60, 62) more rows of fagot patt as established (maintaining first and last st in St st), ending with a WS row.

NEXT ROW (RS): K1, *k2tog, k1, ssk, rep from * to last st, k1—38 (41, 41, 44) sts.

Break yarn. Place rem 38 (41, 41, 44) sts on holder; these will be grafted to corresponding sts from left front to form collar.

back

Transfer rem 97 (107, 117, 127) sts from holder to needle. With WS facing, rejoin yarn and purl 1 row.

Beg with a RS row, cont working in fagot st patt as established (maintaining first and last st in St st) until back measures 9 (9, 10, 10)"/23 (23, 25, 25)cm from underarm, ending with a WS row.

NEXT ROW (RS): K1, *k2tog, k1, ssk, rep from * to last st, k1—59 (65, 71, 77) sts.

NEXT ROW (WS): BO all sts loosely purlwise.

Note
Pieces are blocked, and then waistband is picked up around cast-on edge of body and knitted on. Waistband is worked so that left front overlaps right front; inside of right front is attached to WS after waistband is complete. Block piece.

Waistband
Hold garment with bottom edge at top and RS facing (see Diagram 1). Using smaller needle and beg at front corner of body (A), pick up and knit 1 st in each of next 205 (220, 235, 250) cast-on sts, working around cast-on edge of vest and stopping when 82 (87, 92, 97) cast-on sts rem (B). Place marker and join to work in the rnd.

Note
Remaining portion of right front (B to C) will line up behind left front to form overlapping edge; you will seam these rem 82 (87, 92, 97) sts to WS of work later (see Diagram 2).

Waistband rnd: *K3, p2, rep from * to end.

Rep this rnd eight more times, then BO all sts loosely in ribbing.

With WS facing, seam rem cast-on sts to picked-up front ribbing pieces (segment between B and C) so that left front overlaps right front (see Diagram 2).

Seam shoulders.

Graft 38 (41, 41, 44) live sts from left front (D) to 38 (41, 41, 44) live sts from right front (E) to form collar (see Diagram 1).

Sew collar bottom to back neck, placing grafted center seam at center back and easing in fullness. Weave in rem ends.

Duo Vest Schematic 1

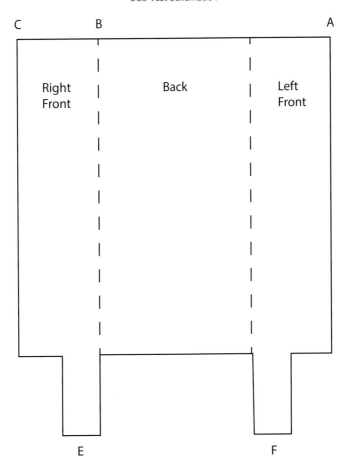

C   B   A

Right Front   Back   Left Front

E   F

Duo Vest Schematic 2

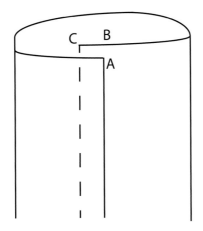

C B

A

KNITTING ABBREVIATIONS

ABBREVIATION	DESCRIPTION	ABBREVIATION	DESCRIPTION	ABBREVIATION	DESCRIPTION	ABBREVIATION	DESCRIPTION
[ ]	work instructions within brackets as many times as directed	g	gram	prev	previous	ss	slip stitch (Canadian)
( )	work instructions within parentheses as many times as directed	inc	increase/increases/ increasing	psso	pass slipped stitch over	ssk	slip, slip, knit these 2 stitches together—a decrease
* *	repeat instructions following the asterisks as directed	k or K	knit	pwise	purlwise	sssk	slip, slip, slip, knit 3 stitches together
*	repeat instructions following the single asterisk as directed	kf & b	knit front and back of same stich	p2tog	purl 2 stitches together	st(s)	stitch(es)
"	inches	kwise	knitwise	rem	remain/remaining	St st	stockinette stitch/ stocking stitch
alt	alternate	k2tog	knit 2 stitches together	rep	repeat(s)	tbl	through back loop
approx	approximately	k3tog	knit 3 stitches together	rev St st	reverse stockinette stitch	tog	together
beg	begin/beginning	k3togtbl	purl 3 stitches together	RH	right hand	w & t	wrap and turn
bet	between	LH	left hand	rnd(s)	round(s)	WS	wrong side
BO	bind off	lp(s)	loop(s)	RS	right side	wyib	with yarn in back
CC	contrasting color	m	meter(s)			wyif	with yarn in front
cm	centimeter(s)	MC	main color	sk	skip	yd(s)	yard(s)
cn	cable needle	mm	millimeter(s)	skp	slip, knit, pass stitch over—one stitch decreased	yfwd	yarn forward
CO	cast on	M1	make 1 stitch	sk2p	slip 1, knit 2 together, pass slip stitch over the knit 2 together; 2 stiches have been decreased	yo	yarn over
cont	continue	M1 p-st	make 1 purl stitch	sl	slip	yon	yarn over needle
dec	decrease/decreases/ decreasing	oz	ounce(s)	sl st	slip stitch(es)	yrn	yarn around needle
dpn	double pointed needle(s)	p or P	purl	sl1k	slip 1 knitwise		
fl	front loop(s)	PM	place marker	sl1p	slip 1 purlwise		
foll	follow/follows/ following	pop	popcorn	sm	slip marker		

YARN WEIGHTS

YARN WEIGHT SYMBOL & CATEGORY NAMES	(0) lace	(1) super fine	(2) fine	(3) light	(4) medium	(5) bulky	(6) super bulky	(7) jumbo
TYPE OF YARNS IN CATEGORY	Fingering 10-count crochet thread	Sock, Fingering, Baby	Sport, Baby	DK, Light Worsted	Worsted, Afghan, Aran	Chunky, Craft, Rug	Bulky, Roving	Jumbo

Source: Craft Yarn Council of America's www.YarnStandards.com

KNITTING NEEDLE SIZE CHART

METRIC (MM)	US	UK/CANADIAN
2.0	0	14
2.25	1	13
2.75	2	12
3.0	—	11
3.25	3	10
3.5	4	—
3.75	5	9
4.0	6	8
4.5	7	7
5.0	8	6
5.5	9	5
6.0	10	4
6.5	10½	3
7.0	—	2
7.5	—	1
8.0	11	0
9.0	13	00
10.0	15	000
12.0	17	—
16.0	19	—
19.0	35	—
25.0	50	—

Acknowledgments

Writing a book is a process, and there are so many people who help in big ways and little along the way. I can't thank my family, Jason, Austin, Caleb, and Peyton, enough. From enduring the myriad of swatches around the house to allowing me to knit through school meetings and sporting events, they have been patient and supportive. Peyton, I thank you for all your color advice! Everyone at Kirkwood Knittery, Robyn and Doug and all the knit night gang, has been with me every step of the way, offering encouragement when needed and silence when required (so I could count my stitches!). A special thanks goes out to Anne Hixson for knitting the Duo scarf.

The unsung heroes of the publishing world are our tech editors, and I am so thankful to Carol Sulcoski for taking on this huge job! Several of the designs in this book feature creative shaping and techniques for assembling, and Carol did an amazing job of putting these features into words that are clear and concise. My editor, Connie Santisteban, has been an amazing source of support and encouragement. Thank you for keeping me on track, for helping me to organize my thoughts, and for all the great advice. I was thrilled to have Carrie Hoge as my photographer again. Thank you for knowing exactly what was in my mind's eye when I created these designs and for showing that through your photos.

Most of all, though, I have to thank my parents, Gene and Shirley Holemon. While they were raising me and my siblings, they never asked, "Did you do your homework?" Not because they didn't care but because it was understood that giving your best effort at all times was a baseline expectation. They led by example, showing us all how to live a full, well-rounded life. My mother shows her artistry in everything she touches, and it has always been my goal to be just like her when I grow up. My father was the wisest man I will ever meet, and in his later years we all were blessed to see his creative side blossom. Thank you both for being role models and giving me the courage and security to always put my best foot forward.

Index

A
Arbor Triangular Shawl, 46–53
Aria Gauntlets, 39–43
Attentive swatching, 10

B
Belly Button cast on, 69, 79
Bind off, lace, 16
Buffalo Wool Company, 113

C
Cast on
    Belly Button, 69, 70
    knit, 11
Circle projects
    Aria Gauntlets, 39–43
    DeBeauliver Top, 26–33
    Mozzetta Capelet, 20–25
    overview of, 19
    Whorl Shawl, 34–37
Cluster stitches
    creating, 13
    for Mozzetta Capelet, 21
Counterpanes, knitted, 69

D
DeBeauliver top, 27–33
Decrease bind off. See Lace bind off

E
Estonian star stitch
    and Holly Shawl, 75
    and Mozzetta Capelet, 14

F
Fagot stitch
    for Duo Vest, 119
    for Uno Cowl, 103
"Fully fashioned shaping," 106

G
Gauge, 10

H
Holly Shawl, 74–83

K
Keira Wrap, 84–87
Knitting abbreviations, 124

Knitting needle size chart, 125
Knitting techniques, lace
    cluster stitches and nupps, 13
    knit cast on, 11
    lace bind off, 16
    short rows, 15, 16
    yarn overs, 12, 13

L
Lace bind off, 16
Lace fabric, 8
Lace knitting techniques
    cluster stitches and nupps, 13
    knit cast on, 11
    lace bind off, 16
    short rows, 15, 16
    yarn overs, 12, 13
Lea Sleeveless Top, 92–99
Log cabin quilts, 75

M
Montauk gauntlets, 41
Montauk Sweater, 62–67
Mozzetta Capelet, 21–25

N
Nupps, 13

P
Peony Tam, 68–71
"PI" shawl, 21
Primrose Tunic, 104–111

R
Rectangle projects
    description of, 101
    Uno Cowl, 102–103
    PrimroseTunic, 104–111
    Troika Wrap, 112–117

S
Shawls
    Amaryliss Entrelac Shawl, 54–61
    Arbor Triangular Shawl, 46–53
    Holly Shawl, 74–83
    Wanderlust Shawl, 88–91

Short rows, 15–16
Sleeveless top, 92–99
Squares projects
    description of, 73
    Duo Vest, 118–123
    Holly Shawl, 74–83
    Keira Wrap, 84–87
    Lea Sleeveless Top, 92–99
    Wanderlust Shawl, 88–91

T
Tams, Peony, 68–71
Triangle projects
    Amaryllis Entrelac Shawl, 54–61
    Arbor Triangular Shawl, 46–53
    designing with, 45
    Montauk Sweater, 62–67
    Peony Tam, 68–71
Troika Wrap, 112–117
Tunic, 104–111

U
Uno Cowl, 102–103

W
Wanderlust Shawl, 88–91
Whorl gauntlets, 41
Whorl shawl, 34–37
Wool-based yarn, 8
Wraps
    Keira Wrap, 84–87
    TroikaWrap, 112–117

Y
Yarn
    a note on, 8
    weights, 125
Yarn overs, 12, 13

Z
Zimmerman, Elizabeth, 21

About the Author

Brooke Nico lives in Kirkwood, MO, a suburb outside St. Louis that has a small-town feel and is a great place to raise kids. It was there that she founded Kirkwood Knittery, which she now runs with business partner Robyn Schrager. A seamstress all her life, Brooke learned to sew her own clothes early to fit her tall, thin frame. In 2000 she taught herself to knit and fell in love with the concept of creating her own fabric while creating a garment. Brooke is the author of *Lovely Knitted Lace: A Geometric Approach to Gorgeous Wearables* (Lark Crafts 2014). Brooke travels and teaches at knitting events around the country, and her designs have been published in *Sock Yarn Studio* (Lark Crafts 2014), *One + One Scarves, Shawls, & Shrugs* (Lark Crafts 2012), *One + One Hats* (Lark Crafts 2012), and *Lace Yarn Studio* (Lark Crafts 2015). Her friends describe her as creative, sharp, and witty. She often talks to her knitting (she swears it answers back!), and she loves shoes, bags, and coffee.